Military Media Management

This book examines the practices of actors involved in the media reportage of war, and the ways in which these practices may influence the conduct of modern military operations.

War is a complex phenomenon which raises numerous questions about the organization of society that continue to challenge all those involved in its study. Increasingly, this includes the need to engage theoretically and empirically with the progressive collapse between the ways in which wars are conducted and the manner in which they are reported in the media.

Drawing on the work of Erving Goffman, *Military Media Management* offers a distinctly new approach to our appreciation of the dynamic relationship between war and media; one that is fundamentally a product of social relations between those engaged in reporting war and those conducting war campaigns. By exploring how and why the military manage information in particular ways, the text succeeds in providing a framework through which wider sociological investigation of this relationship can be understood.

This book will be of much interest to students of military and security studies, media studies, war and conflict studies and IR in general.

Sarah Maltby is a lecturer in sociology and media. She is the founder of the War and Media Network and co-editor of *Communicating War: Memory, Military and Media* (Arima Publishing, 2007). Her research centers on military information management and representations of conflict in military and journalistic output.

Media, War and Security
Series Editors: Andrew Hoskins
University of Glasgow
Oliver Boyd-Barrett,
Bowling Green State University

This series interrogates and illuminates the mutually shaping relationship between war and media as transformative of contemporary society, politics and culture.

Global Terrorism and New Media
The Post Al-Qaeda Generation
Philip Seib and Dana M. Janabek

Radicalisation and the Media
Legitimising Violence in the New Media
Akil N. Awan, Andrew Hoskins and Ben O'Loughlin

Hollywood and the CIA
Cinema, Defense and Subversion
Oliver Boyd-Barrett, David Herrera and Jim Baumann

Violence and War in Culture and the Media
Athina Karatzogianni

Military Media Management
Negotiating the 'Front' Line in Mediatized War
Sarah Maltby

Icons of War and Terror
Media Images in an Age of International Risk
Edited by John Tulloch and R. Warwick Blood

Military Media Management

Negotiating the 'front' line in mediatized war

Sarah Maltby

Routledge
Taylor & Francis Group

LONDON AND NEW YORK

First published 2012
by Routledge
711 Third Avenue, New York, NY 10017

Simultaneously published in the UK
by Routledge
2 Park Square, Milton Park, Abingdon, Oxon OX14 4RN

Routledge is an imprint of the Taylor & Francis Group, an informa business

First issued in paperback 2013

British Library Cataloguing in Publication Data
A catalogue record for this book is available from the British Library

Library of Congress Cataloging-in-Publication Data
Maltby, Sarah.
Military media management : negotiating the "front" line in mediatized war / Sarah Maltby.
    p. cm.
    Includes bibliographical references and index.
    1. Armed Forces and mass media–Great Britain. 2. Great Britain–
    Armed Forces–Public relations. 3. War–Press coverage–Great Britain.
    I. Title.
    P96.A752G75 2012
    070.4'4935500941–dc23   2011040910

ISBN: 978-0-415-58005-2 (hbk)
ISBN: 978-0-415-73129-4 (pbk)
ISBN: 978-0-203-12285-3 (ebk)

Typeset in Times New Roman
by Wearset Ltd, Boldon, Tyne and Wear

Contents

Acknowledgements

For many reasons this book has been a number of years in the making. For as many reasons, there are a number of people to whom I am indebted and without whom this book would not have been possible.

I am extremely grateful to Andrew Hoskins and Oliver Boyd-Barrett as Series Editors for their belief in the book and their invaluable editorial guidance. I am also thankful to all those from the military and media communities who gave their time so willingly to participate in the research, especially David Hudson.

I have been immensely fortunate to be surrounded by colleagues whose support and intellectual stimulation have been a constant source of encouragement. In particular, I would like to thank Kevin McSorley, Helen Thornham, Andrew Hoskins, Ben O'Loughlin, Richard Keeble, Lucy Robinson and Mike Bracken for variously indulging my ideas and providing crucial feedback when it was most needed. Special thanks also to Martin Innes and Geoff Cooper for their early guidance, academic inspiration and for alerting me (in Goffmanesque terms) to the fact that I should never take up poker. I would also like to acknowledge all the members of the War and Media Network for their continued enthusiasm, and to Kurt Beers for his efficiency in helping to manage the network.

Thank you to friends, including some of those above, whose steadfast loyalty and support during the last ten years has contributed to the completion of this book in more ways than they could know. A special thanks to Lucy and Simon Brooks whose friendship I value beyond measure, and to Hamish Wheeler whose tenacious questioning of the world is both edifying and inspirational. Finally, I am indebted to my family's exceptional care and patience, at times against the odds. In particular, I would like to thank Bryan and Susan Maltby for their unfaltering encouragement of my ambitions and for providing me with everything I might need to realize them.

I dedicate this book to Bryan Maltby for helping me – in every way – to seize those opportunities that his own mother was denied; may your lines always be tight Dad.

1 Introduction

War is a complex phenomenon raising numerous questions about the organization of social life which continue to challenge all those involved in its study. Increasingly, this includes the need to engage theoretically and empirically with the progressive collapse between the ways wars are conducted and the ways they are reported in the media. This book is a contribution to the continued and necessary scholarly engagement with this field of investigation. Based on ethnographic research conducted with the British military and British broadcasters between 2001 and 2010, it aims to provide a sociologically informed understanding of the motivations and processes apparent in the management of information about military operations *by* the military *for* the media. In so doing, it recognizes that a more general and theoretically informed framework is needed to understand the organizational structures and information management practices of the relevant agencies involved in the media reportage of war, and the ways in which these practices may influence the conduct of modern military operations.

Of course, there has long been scholarly engagement with the relationship between war and media. Indeed, for many the events of 9/11 represented a turning point in world politics and the organization of war characterized by the US/UK deployments in Afghanistan and Iraq, and the perceived threat of terrorism. As a result, academic evaluations of the war and media relationship, ranging across media and cultural studies, sociology, international relations and war studies have perhaps been at their most fervent in the last decade. Many of these have made valuable contributions to the debate. Most, however, have focused on critiques of political and military 'propaganda' strategies (or media complicity with them); the journalistic experience of war reportage; or the media coverage of war (see, in particular, Thussu and Freedman, 2003; Allan and Zelizer, 2004; Tumber and Palmer, 2004; Miller, 2004; Wilcox, 2005; Tumber and Webster, 2006; Moorcroft and Taylor, 2008; Robinson *et al.*, 2010; Keeble and Mair, 2010). Consequently, analyses of media practice and the impact of the military strategies on media practice have tended to dominate the field. While there is some specialist literature that explicitly explores military–media relations, and which offers unique insights into military practice, much of this literature is either historically driven, or lacks coherent theoretical argument (see Badsey, 1994, 1996, 2000, 2001; Rid, 2007; Tatham, 2006; Taylor, 1992, 1996, 2000, 2003).

Indeed, this is true of much (although not all) of the war and media literature that has tended to evaluate military media management through chronological analyses of wars against dichotomized themes of control vs. cooperation. Hence, for most, the Vietnam War is the first benchmark against which military media management is measured, because US defeat was largely attributed to uncensored media reportage (Carruthers, 2000; Badsey, 1994; see also Hallin, 1989; Braestrup, 1983). In contrast, the constrictive media management during the Falklands/Malvinas conflict represents the second benchmark, where extreme military censorship and information control was considered to preclude journalistic independence (Foster, 1992; Glasgow University Media Group, 1985; Morrison and Tumber, 1988; Adams, 1986). Operating within the shadow of these 'benchmarks', and in the growing recognition that the media can play a vital role in the success or failure of a war campaign, some commentators stress that military–media relations are now fundamentally oriented to cooperation (rather than censorship) and open information policies (Badsey, 1994; Taylor, 2000). Indeed, Dandeker (2000) argues that this critical shift in military thinking – from a position of hostile censorship to one of public relations – has been driven by recognition that more sophisticated approaches are needed. For others, however, the shift from the explicit censorship to one of apparent transparency is merely an indication of how militaries have become more manipulative in their media management strategies, precisely to avoid accusations of control. Thrall (2000), for instance, argues that military media management is now founded on minimizing access to the battle space (and hence information) while maximizing control through other means, specifically the employment of maneuvers that are difficult for the media to verify. Others have suggested that systems like embedding, which provide unprecedented media access to military action, are actually designed to stifle dissent among journalists in order that the military can set the media agenda (Schechter, 2003; Tumber and Palmer, 2004; Couldry and Downing, 2004; Lewis and Brookes, 2004). In this way, embedding is seen as a deliberate strategy designed to seduce both journalist and viewer with apparent facticity while detracting attention from the wider political and moral context of the war (Keeble, 2004).

These insights are valuable in their critique of military (and state) practice, and highlight the degree to which the media are increasingly utilized as a resource in the legitimization of war campaigns. At the same time, their almost exclusive focus on the ways in which the militaries or governments attempt to control and restrict information for the media inadequately express the complexities of the military–media relationship. Few scholars, for instance, have theoretically engaged with the effect of the media on military institutional practice, despite the growing body of work dedicated to the effect of structural and bureaucratic processes of media institutions on the practice of other institutions, particularly the police (see, in particular, Doyle, 2003; Manning, 2003; Schlesinger and Tumber, 1994; Ericson *et al.*, 1989, 1991; Hall *et al.*, 1978). Those who have, particularly Cottle (2006) and Hoskins and O'Loughlin (2010), offer important and significant insights into the influence of the media on the conduct of war, but posit their arguments in broad theoretical analysis that does not elucidate the nuances of military practice, especially why and how militaries orient their war conduct to the media in particular ways.

The intention of this book is to draw upon all these analyses, but move beyond them to empirically ground the explicit and implicit information management that *both* the military and the media bring to bear on the production of war news, and the consequences of these practices for the conduct of war. Thus, rather than considering the activities of the military and the media as distinct, here they are understood as merging to the point where they become integral to each other (see Schulz, 2004). This does not preclude the emergence of cooperation or conflict in the military–media relationship. Instead, this book examines why, how and when conflict and cooperation emerges to better understand why and how militaries organize their practices with the media in mind.

In this way, the changing nature of warfare is relevant to the broader context in which these practices take place. Wars, certainly for Western states, can no longer be contained or won by kinetic force alone. This has long been recognized in the variously conceptualized notion of 'information warfare', which although devoid of a single consensual definition, in its simplest form is the struggle for control and dominance over information and information systems in a manner that marginalizes other, more traditional, forms of warfare (Libicki, 1995). Characterized by an increasing military reliance on information, electronic and global communication systems, the use of intelligence, deception, and perception management have become vital in the conduct of war (Hirst, 2001; Molander *et al.*, 1996; Ventre, 2009). In part, this is due to the declining optimism associated with the technological advances of the 'Revolution in Military Affairs' (RMA). These have been all but overshadowed by everyday dependence upon, and interdependence of, globalized economic, commercial and political infrastructures that have created a new frontier for war (Molander *et al.*, 1996; Libicki, 1995). In recognition of the power and vulnerability of these globally interconnected infrastructures, information – rather than kinetic force – is now considered the dominant weapon of war. Moreover, the growth of asymmetric warfare – most evident in those activities collectively termed 'insurgency' and 'terrorism' and what Downey and Murdock (2003) term a 'counter revolution in military affairs' – has accentuated the potential impotence of advanced weaponry systems and kinetic force.

The intensification of asymmetric warfare and the processes of globalization are not, however, necessarily unrelated. Globalization can exclude and disconnect a substantial proportion of the world's population. For some, this unequal distribution of power creates fertile ground for violent resistance to – and the challenging of universal principles that accompany – globalization, including democracy and secular capitalism (Giddens, 1988a; Bauman, 1997; Castells, 2000). Within this perspective, the intensification of asymmetric warfare and the development of information warfare both result from the conditions of globalization, creating motivation for conflict, *and* a means through which it can be expressed. In response, and in the realization that war cannot be won with technology alone, information has been brought to the forefront of strategic thinking for all those conducting war. It is now, simultaneously, both a target and a weapon. Essentially, as militaries attempt to impose their will through the influence, manipulation and prohibited access to information, information *becomes* the war (Schwartau, 1994; Toffler and Toffler, 1980; Toffler, 1991). Consequently, the ability to influence perceptions – and thus behavior – for those conducting and experiencing war has become critical to pursing a competitive advantage over an adversary.

Under these conditions, perception management and influence in and through the media are no longer isolated components of a war campaign – as was traditionally the case – but rather the campaign itself. As Hoskins and O'Loughlin (2010: 5) point out, it is through the media that perceptions are created, sustained and challenged. The media are *the* decisive means of mass communication in which one needs a presence to have presence in the public mind (Castells, 2009). The ability to achieve political or social influence thus becomes synonymous with the ability to convey one's message(s) through the media. As Cottle (2006) argues, we live in mediatized times where everyone looks to the media to advance their strategic aims. This is more than just mediation, however (Hjarvard, 2008a). Ultimately, it requires social and political actors to orient their communicative strategies and working practices toward the needs and interests of media organizations; to the logic of the media (Altheide and Snow, 1979). A consequence of this is the merging and converging of war and media practices to a point where distinctions become difficult. Essentially, war becomes defined, justified, legitimated and ultimately fought through and with the media. In this way, the convergence of war and media practice can be situated within broader arguments about the integral role of the media in the formation and practice of *all* social, cultural and political institutions.

For many, the growth of media influence is now so all-encompassing that society has been fundamentally transformed as a result; everyday practices and social relations are shaped by mediating technologies and media organizations (Livingstone, 2009a). This has been termed 'mediatization', in which contemporary complex conditions could not be enacted or managed without the media. In this way, mediatization shapes society as well as the relationships that individuals and institutions have to their environment and each other (Silverstone, 2005). For Hjarvard (2008a), mediatization is a long-lasting process through which institutions and their modes of interaction are changed to accommodate the role of the media and its powerful, influential communicative properties; they are 'mediatized'. In these conditions, the media have a fundamental influence on how and why war and military actions are performed in particular ways. As a concept, mediatization thus allows us to theorize the convergence of war and media as a recognized outcome of the increasing influence of mass media in contemporary society. For Hoskins and O'Loughlin, then, mediatized war is where war is reconstituted as a result of the processes of mediatization, precisely because the 'planning, waging and consequences of warfare do not reside outside the media' (2010: 5).

Few, however, have clarified the mediatizing processes that lead to the convergence of war and media (Livingstone, 2009a; McQuail, 2006). Thus, the ways in which militaries understand, organize and execute war actions in and through the media is of critical importance if we are to better understand the empirical reality of mediatized war for those engaged in it. For example, many have commented on the cyclical process whereby military and media actions mutually feed into, and influence, the subsequent actions of the other party. Yet the focus tends to be on the ways this impacts upon the media. In this regard, it is the media, cognizant that war is increasingly designed for media presentational purposes, who orient their own practices toward these designs for their own purposes (see Hoskins and O'Loughlin, 2010). Few, however, have considered in any depth the degree to which the military may be engaging in the same reflexive processes and whether this fundamentally alters militarist performances? Do they also, for instance, interpret, orient and reorient their actions to accommodate media management practices; if so, how, when and to what end? If, as Cottle (2008) suggests, mediatizing techniques can fundamentally affect the outcome of war, then interrogating the ways in which militaries understand their own position in relation to the media is of critical importance.

Moreover, this raises subsidiary, but important, questions regarding how militaries conceive of their audiences with regard to mediated communications, and the role of the audience in the organization of military action. Beyond the recognition that political and moral legitimacy is sought from audiences through media reportage, there is little empirical or theoretical consideration, for instance, of *who* militaries may be attempting to communicate with and why. Do they, for instance, draw upon the media to achieve objectives other than political legitimation, such as internal political leverage, the mobilization of potential recruits, or the acceleration of an adversary's defeat? And, if so, who are the audiences among whom these actions may be elicited? The role of the audience has tended to be a comparatively neglected aspect in studies of war and media, usually only referred to occasionally, and typically framed in terms of passive spectatorship. Of course, there is now an emergent body of literature that more comprehensively engages with the impact of coverage on audiences and the public consciousness, and the variable interpretations they bring to the text (Hoskins, 2004; Gillespie, 2006; Hoskins and O'Loughlin, 2007, 2010). These contributions are noteworthy because of the ways in which they conceptualize the audience as part of an ongoing process through which media texts are produced and interpreted. The work contained within this book draws parallels with these works by exploring how the military may use the notion of 'audience' as a construct to organize and produce media output for their own aims. In so doing, the book attempts to elucidate some of the nuances of mediatized war by considering audiences in the formulation of military actions.

The utility of Goffman

In an attempt to interrogate some of these issues, this book empirically grounds the information management practices of the British military in Goffman's (1959, 1969) theory of impression management and strategic information management. Located within the symbolic interactionist tradition, Goffman's work gives particular attention to face-to-face interaction and small-scale social contexts. While the relationship between Goffman's sociology and symbolic interactionism is a source of continuing debate,[1] for Goffman (and other symbolic interactionists), the everyday world is a product of human subjectivity that is reified when it is forgotten and taken for granted. This position assumes that social reality derives from ways in which individuals define, interpret and give meaning to their world. It also assumes that in order for those meanings to be meaningful, they must be shared, learned and communicated through symbolic exchanges and interactions. Because much of this symbolic exchange is implicit, symbolic interactionists have traditionally studied the social world from the standpoint of the individual(s) involved. Such an approach – usually referred to as ethnomethodology – allows for the investigation of the ways individuals order, share and produce their social world through their own interpretations and the meanings they ascribe to situations (Garfinkel, 1967). As William Isaac Thomas so famously stated, 'If men define situations as real, they are real in their consequences.' It is within this methodological framework that Goffman attempted to uncover the implicit knowledge that individuals acquire and use in social interaction.

Although primarily concerned with individual identity and self-presentation, Goffman's analysis is able to offer valuable insights into the nature of meaningful social interaction with, and among, larger institutions and society. In his focus on the detail of unremarkable everyday interactions, he invokes the remarkable by revealing the implicit knowledge involved in interaction, one that is rarely articulated because of its habitual nature. As a result, Goffman illuminates our understanding of the symbolic value of what is said and done *by* actors *for* actors, allowing us to deepen our understanding of how the social world is produced and reproduced through social relations. Like the concept of mediatization, a Goffmanesque perspective draws attention to the micro social world, allowing us to connect it to macro social systems (Giddens, 1988b; see also Lundby, 2009). Of course, some have argued that Goffman's micro approach to sociological analysis reflects a disinterest in power and hierarchy (Gouldner, 1970). Yet, Goffman's deep analysis of influence and control, particularly relevant to the work contained here, is demonstrative of how power is inherent in all aspects of his work (Rogers, 1980). By investigating and challenging 'taken for granted' assumptions in social interaction, Goffman allows us to see beyond individuals to interrogate similar assumptions in power structures, and institutional actions like war. Thus, although Smith (1999) has criticized Goffman's work for its fragmentary nature, his methods and analyses continue to be utilized and developed by many of his interpreters interested in macro power relations

(Johansson, 2009). This is one such work. It builds upon and transfers Goffman's ideas about interpersonal relations – particularly the dramaturgical perspective in which actors attempt to achieve influence and credibility through impression management – from individual interactions to the level of organizations and publics. In so doing, it seeks to illuminate how and why militaries organize war in particular ways, for and through the media, and the degree to which this is related to a desire (or need) to influence others.

By situating the military and their media management practices in this perspective, the convergence of war conduct and its reportage becomes located within interactions between the military and the media. Goffman's (1969) notion of strategic interaction, as a sequence of moves, counter-moves and adaptations becomes a means through which we can understand how militaries attempt to control what is acquired, revealed and concealed about their activities in the pursuit of these broader objectives. This symbolic interactionist perspective has particular utility in furthering our understanding of the phenomenon of mediatized war as fundamentally a product of social relations between those engaged in reporting war, and those conducting war campaigns. As Lundby (2009) suggests, because mediatizing processes are intensified in war and conflict, they become more visible. This book is thus an attempt to empirically ground these processes in Goffman's dramaturgical perspective in order to better elucidate them. In so doing, it also aims to contribute to, and develop upon, the growing body of work dedicated to the study of mediatization.

Researching the British military

There are a number of factors that informed the research process with the British military that contextualize the discussion of military practice in the remainder of this book. These are pertinent for discussion, not least because they afford the reader some insight into the rationale and constraints of the research process, and the methodological implications of such a project.

Due to the nature of the sociological enquiry, data were collected through the combined methods of qualitative interviews, ethnographic fieldwork and textual analysis. Interviews were especially suitable for gaining insights into military members' attitudes, opinions and motivations, thereby elucidating members' understandings of 'what they think they do' (May, 2001). Moreover, by virtue of their need to explain their bureaucratic and organizational systems (and the formulation of individual actions into collective military action) to the 'non-specialist' researcher, the interviews also yielded insights into *why the military do what they think they do*. This latter aspect of the interview method derived from a symbolic interactionist orientation to the research to gain a deeper understanding of how the processes of military media management were perceived to impact upon other military actions. Interviews were conducted with those who engaged with the practice of media management from across the military hierarchy. In addition to these interviews, ethnographic observation was employed to yield insights into 'what respondents do' (rather than what they say they do).

This comprised the bulk of the data collected. In all the fieldwork settings, field-work was conducted in an 'observer as participant' role in which the researcher is engaged in the setting but not taking part in activities that would constitute membership (Gold, 1958; Adler and Adler, 1998). This was intentional in order to maintain a neutral and objective position. It enabled opportunities to uncover some of the taken-for-granted assumptions that military members attach to their actions, particularly in the collective design, communication and interrogation of their actions for particular purposes.

This combined data was triangulated (as much as possible) with television footage, military documents and interviews with television broadcasters. Thus, in a shift away from the dominant orientation that analyzes a television text's representative properties or the reader's experience of the text, here the text was conceived as an artifact that was expressive of the structured relationships and organizational processes (both in and between military and media institutions) that informed its construction. The television text was not therefore considered in isolation, but as a product of the processes of military media management and the relations between the military and the media that inform these proc-esses. In this respect, television texts were considered no different from other documents in that they were representative of the context and cultural values in (and beyond) the organizational setting, and reflexive of the processes that pro-duced them (Altheide, 1996; Atkinson and Coffey, 1997). This combined approach of qualitative interviews, observational fieldwork and analysis of textual data was employed in an attempt to understand the institutionally derived actions of the military, in accordance with the symbolic meanings they attach to these actions.

At the outset of the research process in early 2001, initial access to the British military was made through a contact who, at the time, was serving in the British Army and based at the Joint Services Command and Staff College (JSCSC).[2] He subsequently left the Army in 2002, but in the meantime acted as a 'gatekeeper' and enabled research access to the JSCSC. At that time, the JSCSC educational remit included military media management training, specifically designed to introduce officers to the subject of Media Operations and provide them with basic media management techniques. This came to be the first fieldwork setting. After 2002, a combined strategy of purposeful and snowball sampling was employed, in which contacts secured at JSCSC were used to enhance access and select fieldwork settings that would be information-rich (Patton, 1990).

Drawing on these sampling methods, new gatekeepers and fieldwork settings were secured. By 2010 data had been collected from a total of seven fieldwork settings. Two of these were media management training sessions, both prior to and after the onset of the Iraq War. Of course, by their nature, these settings are centrally organized around how the military can *successfully* manage the media. This has the potential to be markedly different from how the media is managed in operational scenarios. As such, the data collected were manifestly a guide for military impression management action rather than an indication of action itself. In this way, the training setting provided data regarding what the military say they will do in a given situation while not actually in it. Although this provides crucial insight into military thinking, there can be a disparity between what people say and what they do (Deutscher, 1973). It was therefore difficult to investigate in any depth the problems that may be encountered in the actual practice of military management based on these settings alone. Although the military used examples taken from prior experience to illustrate problems that arise, these were purposefully selected and restricted to what they considered to be the most salient issues for training purposes. In order to effectively overcome this dilemma, consideration was given to embarking on an ethnographic project in situ with the military during actual operations. While the British military made such an opportunity available during the early stages of this research process – through an invitation to shadow Media Operations work in Iraq – it was eventually considered by all parties concerned that, at that stage, the benefits of such an undertaking were outweighed by the risks of conducting research in such a volatile environment. Thus, it was important to find other field settings that would offer insight into the actual practice of military media management, but without the risk of an operational environment. As a result, a number of other field settings were secured, which consisted of either formal structured meetings, conferences, military news management desks based in the United Kingdom and informal visits to military settings (such as the MoD). In addition, and often by virtue of the longevity of some of these 'field visits', there were a number of other informal, social settings (such as mealtimes) that provided insight into military members' experiences of, or more informal perspectives on, media management.

It is important at this stage to highlight that because the British military were not engaged in operations at the genesis of the project in early 2001, the research focused on the more generic processes of institutional information management. After 9/11, however, and with the British military deployment to Afghanistan and Iraq, the management of media information during conflict operations become the basis of an ongoing study. The advantage, as with a case-study approach, was the ability to explore in depth the processes and practices of both institutions in relation to the social context of these wars. The immediacy with which information became available therefore offered new insights into a topic of both historical and contemporary relevance. More significant, however, was the ability to collect data about the British military's media management practices both prior to and during major combat operations; and in the case of Iraq within a month of these operations ending. This was an interesting and unique aspect of the research, particularly because the military themselves were reflexive about their media management practices in Iraq and the implications for the future.

Perhaps the biggest 'trade off' in gaining such unique access to the military was that the data could only be collected under terms in which no information could be quoted or accredited to particular military personnel (unless already in the public domain). Consequently, throughout this book findings are referenced with a footnote highlighting their source (i.e. date of ethnographic work or interview). It is acknowledged that there are limitations to this form of referencing data, not least the inability to provide the reader with clear empirical examples, such as discursive quotes. Indeed, anticipating that this would be particularly restrictive in the writing process, a research strategy was employed to actively seek information in the public domain with which to triangulate the military data and from which quotes could be used. To this end, military documents located through the MoD's website became especially significant because they often replicated the discursive ethnographic data pertaining to the aims, pragmatics and structure of media management and the categorization of audiences. Similarly, data from television news and documentaries offered examples of military media management (in action) that could be empirically referred to without compromising adherence to confidentiality. Because the military were engaged in ongoing operations in Iraq and Afghanistan and were often in the news, there were often occasions when they cited situations that were also evident in news reports. At other times, explicit reference was made to television reports in conversation or during interviews to draw out a military perspective on a situation that could later be grounded in existing television data.

Notwithstanding these efforts, it is recognized that an inability to offer the reader clear and concrete examples of findings from the military data is still limiting. Not only are descriptions of the data devoid of nuance, but the reader is also denied the opportunity to interrogate and critically engage with the interpretations made. However, such restrictions are not unique to this particular research group. Most research is constrained in some manner by the conditions under which it can be investigated or presented. This rarely prevents the researcher from embarking on the research and sharing the findings in a manner that will deepen understanding of the phenomenon under investigation. This is one such project.

The conditions imposed, while restricting the ways in which the data can be presented, permitted engagement in an insightful and empirically grounded analysis of military media management practice that would otherwise not have been possible. Thus, the summative nature of the data presented here is a stylistic device through which to present findings that are not only substantiated in rich empirical data, but also obtained from an essentially under-researched institution. In recognition of some of the limitations this summative data presents, however, the discussion below offers further detail of, and reflection upon the research process, from which it is hoped the reader might better appreciate the nature of the research settings

First, while field relations with the military varied according to the contexts of the settings, it became apparent that (overall) military personnel placed a high degree of value on academic research, and on this research in particular. In part, this was due to their desire to learn from the findings. This is not uncommon in ethnographic work, in which respondents wish to 'trade off' their participation with something for themselves (Lofland and Lofland, 1995). While no commitments were made to such a trade off, it was perhaps by virtue of the final rewards on completion of the project that the military permitted a reasonable degree of freedom in the military field settings. At the same time, as the research pro-gressed it became evident that the military's enthusiasm for the research was also motivated by a desire to be perceived as an 'open' institution. This is not a neutral issue for the military. They believe that they come under consistent criti-cism – not least by the media – for being a 'closed' institution and for attempting to control information in and about conflict zones in which they operate. In light of this, and as part of an ongoing process to change public perceptions, their encouragement of academic observation and involvement was, for them, a means through which to demonstrate some form of public accountability. This was made explicit in conversation with a number of military agents. The fact that notions of public accountability were key to respondents' participation in the study became an important empirical finding, not least because it was demon-strative of the degree to which impression management was central to their per-formance of institutional action.

Related to this, and from a dramaturgical perspective, the data collected through ethnographic fieldwork in particular exemplified what Goffman (1959) terms 'back region' action. Hence, military media management practices – typic-ally constructed in the back region – became visible through observational field-work in a manner that was not so tangible via interviews. The data collected was therefore able to elucidate institutional impression management in terms of what was actually done, as opposed to the military's descriptions of what they think they do, which is more commonly associated with the 'front region' action of interviews (Adler and Adler, 1998; see also Goffman, 1959). This distinction is important to understanding institutional impression management and the types of data that are obtainable through different methodologies. For example, although military members discussed 'back region' action in interviews, the interview setting itself became essentially a 'front' for their institutional (and personal) impression management. Indeed, interviewees were less likely to expose the more private aspects of back region work in interviews, such as the ridiculing of the media or other military members.

In contrast, the observational fieldwork made visible those more private aspects of 'back regions', highlighting the considered limitations, frustrations (and perceived triumphs) of media management, the ways in which the military negotiate and construct their actions for the media and the cultural comradeship that frames their collective orientation toward external parties such as the media. While this point is true of all observational fieldwork, it was particularly perti-nent for this research because the focus of these regions was in itself constructed around the need for, and practical workings of, institutional 'back regions' in military media management. Put simply, it was equivalent to interviewing a respondent about the process of being interviewed. This provided crucial insight into the potential disparities between military thinking and doing, which are drawn upon through this book. Moreover, as a researcher engaged in ethno-graphic work, investigating the techniques employed to perform institutional impression management, the need to perform a research 'front' was also integral to the research process (see also Fielding, 1993). This process provided insight into the complexities of the 'performance' world, heightening an appreciation of impression management techniques and strategic interaction necessary to protect one's own informational position.

The final factor essential to the reader's full understanding of the forthcoming discussions is that the perspectives of all those military members who took part in the research are henceforth referred to collectively as the perspectives of 'the military'. There are two reasons for this. The first is a practical one related to the identification of sources, which can be overcome by using a collective term. The second, and more important, reason derives from the ways in which British military members discursively refer to their own military organization as a collective one. Despite the existence of various departments and units in the British military institution, the Joint Services approach to the military was the dominant one expressed during this research process. The Joint Services approach was developed in 1994; under this approach all single-service armed forces (Navy, Air Force and Army), joined to form a tri-service group in order to develop a common understanding of warfare and defense approaches. As specified in the 1998 Strategic Defence Review:

> While single-Service skills and ethos will remain the essential foundation of all our military capability, most future operations will be conducted by joint forces composed of fighting units from individual Services. These will be under joint (tri-Service) command and control, drawing on joint intelligence capabilities and with joint logistics. We must therefore also build the joint approach into our doctrine and our preparation and training for operations; in many areas, support functions can also be most effectively provided on a defence-wide basis.
>
> (Strategic Defence Review, 1998: 30)

This approach was reflected in the development of Joint Services Staff colleges and is further evident in the predominantly unified approach among armed forces personnel. Throughout the research process, members from the military (including members from single services, the Territorial Army and the MoD) consistently referred to themselves collectively as 'we', particularly when discussing operational objectives. In this sense, their own articulations of their organization can be understood in accordance with Mead's (1967) notion of institutions, which he defines as a system of beliefs and practices in which participants incorporate not only their own attitudes and roles, but also the attitudes and roles of all the other participants. To this end, all participants are referred to collectively here as 'the military'.

Of course, this assumes a level of coherence and unity among all military personnel with regard to the motivation and formulation of military work. This can obscure the complexities and divergences apparent in a large, hierarchical and multi-faceted organization, such as the British military, where the meaning attributed to particular actions can vary considerably at different levels of the command structure. Individual action does not always manifestly cohere with the institutional approach, nor does the image of the institution that the military might wish to portray always cohere with actual action. Despite this, the military's own discursive categorization of their organization – certainly with reference to media management – is predominantly one that is collectively unified and oriented toward achieving the same aims.

For this reason, this institutional perspective has some validity as a tool for understanding military media management precisely because it is how the British military conceptualize and present themselves in their media management work. In particular, a collective understanding and orientation to military work is inculcated in the training and socialization of service personnel throughout their careers. Hence, all ranks of military members will consistently invoke the unified institutional approach in their presentations to the media, speaking on behalf of the institution rather than themselves. In so doing, the military present themselves as a unified 'whole' because they wish to be judged as such. Moreover, media discourse does the same, predominantly referring to military members as an institutional body. Individual members are rarely considered as distinct from the institution. Instead, the media employ terms like 'British soldiers', 'members of the British Army' or 'the British military state that', etc.

Certainly, the media can – and do – identify the actions of individual service personnel in controversial or illegal situations. However, the fact that the military refer to this type of action as exceptional or an anomaly is itself indicative of how important a coherent, institutionalized front is to military work. 'Anomalies' that result from fractures in the cohered image of the institution thus offer some insight into the complexities that exist in the military's management of their image. Indeed, Goffman's (1959) alertness to the distinction between front and back regions in interpersonal interactions is an especially useful conceptual tool with which to understand this. It allows us to consider how, collectively, members of an institution work to produce a public image of themselves from which they stand to gain, but which can concurrently be threatened by the realities of their work. Ultimately, while the actions of individual military members may vary, the ongoing cohesiveness with which they attempt to construct their approach to their work, and their own collective use of 'we' in these approaches, is both relevant and important. As such, the collective term of 'the military' employed in this book is reflective of the dominant view that was expressed by those taking part.

Outline of the chapters

In an attempt to be sensitive to the reader's potential unfamiliarity with British military practice, the forthcoming chapters are structured in a linear manner to introduce the reader to the practice of military media management before discussing *why* it is important to the military and the success of an operation, and *how* it is enacted as a means with which to achieve those objectives. For this reason, Chapter 2 provides a brief overview of the current structure and organization of British military media management, termed 'Media Operations'.

The chapter is intended to provide the reader with an appreciation of the form and content of Media Operations work on which all subsequent chapters are based. Chapter 3 then considers the organization of Media Operations in more detail to explain and interrogate the divergence and similarities between academic appreciation of military actions and the motivations and practices of the British military institution itself. In particular, the discussion situates Media Operations within the larger structure of the military institution as both a government-resourced and -directed institution accountable to Parliament and the electorate, *and* an institution with its own goals, rules, culture, identity and working practices.

Chapter 4 lays the theoretical foundations through which Media Operations will be interrogated throughout the remainder of the book, describing how and why Media Operations work can be understood in accordance with Goffman's (1959) notion of impression management. This framework provides the basis for subsequent chapters that interrogate why and how the military define and perform war actions for the media in particular ways. In so doing, the chapter highlights the utility of symbolic interactionism as an encompassing framework through which the differing motivations and strategies of military media management at all levels – from political to tactical – can be understood in accordance with the meanings the military attach to their own actions and those of others.

The remainder of the book is then concerned with the form and organization of military impression management. Chapter 5 explores *why* the military attempt to define their activities in particular ways, and for whom. To this end, a key distinction will be made between military 'audiences' as recipients of military definitions, and 'media observers' as communicators of military definitions. The chapter describes how the military conceive of multiple, heterogeneous audiences when managing information for the media and how the differentiation between each audience group is critical to an appreciation of how, when constructing definitions of their actions, the military are attempting to communicate specific messages simultaneously to different audiences to achieve particular aims.

Chapters 6–9 are concerned with *how* the military attempt to achieve Media Operations objectives through impression management, and the implications of their performances on the conduct of modern military operations. It is within these chapters that Goffman's theory of strategic interaction is introduced. In order to guide the reader through the nuances of military media management, the chapters employ an artificial distinction between 'defining situations' in, and the 'performance of', Media Operations. While, in reality, the defining of a situation is intrinsically linked to the impression management performance, the distinction made in these chapters permits a clearer assessment of how the military proactively and reactively explain and account for their activities.

With this in mind, Chapter 6 is centrally concerned with exploring the ways in which the British military construct *definitions* of their activities, both visually and linguistically, in a manner that is accessible for audiences while meeting the information-gathering needs of the media. Chapter 7 then examines the degrees to which the military fail and succeed in their ability to define situations on their own terms, and the perceived implications for their ongoing activities. Chapters 8 and 9 focus upon how the military attempt to secure the communication of their definitions in the media through both bounded and distanciated impression management. Bounded impression management is the focus of Chapter 8 and is characterized by co-present, or face-to-face impression management, performed in direct interaction with the media through facilities such as press conferences and embedding. It is here that the military attempt to control what is revealed and concealed about their activities. Chapter 9 explores distanciated impression management performed in accordance with Meyrowitz's concept of the 'information system' in which the increased potential for audiences to gain access to information about the actions of the military correlates with the military's diminished capacity to control the performance. Distanciated impression management is therefore concerned with distinguishing and managing impressions of military activity that are intended to be observed and those that are unavoidably observable. It is within this chapter that the mediatization of war becomes evident in the degree to which militaries take account of the potential for their actions to be reported in the media and consequently incorporate performative aspects in their strategic and tactical battle plans.

Lastly, Chapter 10 highlights how Goffman's theories of impression management and strategic interaction have particular utility in providing an encompassing sociological theoretical framework with which to explore the relationship between war and media, providing a unique contribution to existing understandings of how this relationship may be constituted. In so doing, the notion of mediatized war – in which the practice of war is enacted through, involves, and is dependent upon media reportage – is clarified and expanded upon.

2   What are Media Operations?

'Media Operations' is the term used by the British military to describe the management of information about, or related to, British military activities made available to the media. It is one of a number of military information-based activities that have developed significantly over the last two decades. This chapter provides a descriptive overview of the structure and organization of British military Media Operations based on official military documents and military accounts. It therefore employs much of the language utilized by the military through which they articulate the intentions behind, and organization of, Media Operations work. Such a discussion provides crucial insight into military media management. At the same time, it must be borne in mind that disparities exist between these official articulations and how media management is actually performed (Deutscher, 1973). These disparities will be considered in later chapters. For the moment, the description contained here affords the reader an appreciation of the form and content of Media Operations work as articulated by the military themselves, and on which all subsequent analysis is based.

The British military is a complex organization engaged in activities at a diplomatic, political and military level in accordance with the British government's political directives. Military force is not applied in isolation, but is in fact one of three key instruments of national power (the others being economic and diplomatic power). Increasingly, it is argued that information is intrinsic to all three of these powers for them to be effective (JDP (Joint Doctrine Publication), 2008; Taverner, 2007). Consequently, they are all directed by the British government's Information Strategy, which aims to 'influence decisions, opinions and outcomes in order to support the National Strategic Aim and associated policy objectives' (JDP 3-45.1, 2007: 1–2). These objectives are devised and developed in negotiations between government departments, including the Cabinet Office, the Foreign and Commonwealth Office, the Department for International Development and the MoD.

In conflict situations, the objectives of the Information Strategy are fundamentally oriented toward reassuring publics, including allied nations, of the benefits of particular political and military action while 'coercing', 'isolating' or 'undermining' the enemy into defeat (JWP (Joint Warfare Publication) 3-80, 2002: 1-4). Media Operations are the military component of this strategy, aimed at communicating strategic themes and messages to identified audiences in an effort to achieve identified outcomes (JDP 3-45.1, 2007: 1-3; JWP 3-45, 2001: 1-1). More specifically, according to doctrine the overriding objective of Media Operations is to harness and promote 'widespread understanding' of military operations and to generate political and public support. It is precisely defined as:

> That line of activity developed to ensure timely, accurate, and effective pro-vision [through the media] of Public Information (P Info) and implementa-tion of Public Relations (PR) policy within the operational environment, whilst maintaining Operational Security (OPSEC).
>
> (JDP 3-45-1, 2007: 1-3)

Media Operations work is thus founded upon two central, and related, aims. The first is to proactively attempt to secure positive coverage of both the military organization and its activities in line with the strategic objectives of the Informa-tion Strategy and the operational aims of the military. The second is to effect-ively respond to, and manage, adverse media coverage of military activities in a manner that will prevent it undermining strategic and operational objectives. For the military, examples of adverse media coverage range from false allegations and leakage of information that threatens operational security to coverage of incidents like breaches of ceasefire, the capture of British service personnel, 'collateral damage', mass casualties or defeat in battle.[1] Essentially, proactive engagement with the media is considered key to securing positive coverage and managing adverse coverage. Accordingly, military doctrine stresses that success-ful Media Operations must be sensitive to media needs; must treat all media even-handedly; and must only offer information that is accurate and truthful (JDP 3-45.1, 2007: 1-4).

The organizational structure of Media Operations reflects both the political and military aspects of Media Operations work across three differentiated levels: strategic (political), operational (political and military) and tactical (military).

The strategic level takes place in the MoD in London, UK. In the MoD, the Director General of Media and Communications is responsible for all areas of internal and external communications work related to military activity, including the development of the Information Strategy.

The operational level of media information management is conducted in the Permanent Joint Headquarters (PJHQ) in Northwood, UK. PJHQ is a military headquarters responsible for the planning, execution and command of all UK-led, and joint, combined and multinational military operations and includes a Media Operations branch. The operational level of media management at PJHQ is distinct from the strategic in that it is operationally driven but incorporates a strategic component. The PJHQ Media Operations branch is responsible for translating strategic directives into deliverable operational plans relevant to a given battle space.

The tactical level of media information management takes place in the Joint Task Force Headquarters (JTFHQ) in the battle space, termed either the Joint

Area of Operations (JOA) or the theater of operations (see JDP 3-45.1, 2007). JTFHQ are responsible for the practical planning and implementation of PJHQ's directives through a number of different operational substructures, or 'desks', each responsible for various operational needs (such as logistics or artillery).

One of these is a Media Operations 'desk', operated by military Media Operations staff. Their key role is to advise, update and assist an operational commander in their dealings with the media. This involves monitoring of media coverage, briefing military personnel, coordinating information and devising rebuttal material (although rebuttal is primarily carried out at MoD level). In addition, Media Operations staff are responsible for the logistical planning and implementation of Media Operations work, including establishing press information centers, organizing facilities, organizing escorts and producing press information. While the dominant pattern of communication throughout this structure is vertical – allowing strategic directives to be directed down for tactical execution – structural lines of communication permitting upward flows of information are considered imperative because the media can request information at all levels of the structure simultaneously.

Military interaction with the media generally takes place at two central points in the organizational structure: the MoD and the theater of operations. At the strategic level the MoD provide press conferences and background briefings for the media. In the theater of operations, direct interaction between Media Operations staff occurs within three man facilities. Each facility differs in terms of the perceived opportunities it presents for media management and the communication of specific types of information.

The first is the Press Information Centre (PIC), which is considered the focal point for day-to-day military interaction with the media in the theater of operations. It is the central means through which Media Operations staff attempt to distribute information about operations and facilitate escorts and visits to media facilities (see below). The military identify the press center as the core means through which they can gauge media interest, identify developing media themes and analyze the effectiveness of their own Media Operations. All media correspondents have to be registered with the British military in order to seek admission to the press center and its facilities. Registration is granted via application to the MoD, but at the discretion of the MoD. Press centers are usually managed 24 hours per day, with a daily routine including regular press briefings, a daily press conference, one-to-one media briefings and frequent internal meetings among military Media Operations staff. The press center is described as providing 'an acceptable interface with the media' and considered to have a major impact on the success or otherwise of the media operation (JDP 3-45.1, 2007: 5-5). The size and scale of the press information center will depend on the military operation and the number of journalists. The military believe that there is a greater likelihood that journalists will attend the facility if it is both accessible and provides good, comfortable facilities. As such, they attempt to locate the press centers in locations that might encourage media engagement with briefings and conferences.[2] At the same time, the location is also dictated by military considerations, including the need to retain operational security and minimize disruption in the military headquarters.

The second point at which Media Operations staff interact with the media is through events or visits arranged for journalists. Often termed 'media facilities', these visits may include equipment displays, visits to hospitals, tours of battle ships or escorts to particular military activities such as humanitarian deliveries or meetings with local civilians. Facilities are organized for the media on an invitation-only basis. When the media demand for facilities exceeds capacity, 'pooling' occurs. Pooling is the term used to describe the sharing of information among media correspondents. In such instances the media are left to select their own representatives to attend the facility and collect information that is then distributed among all registered journalists (JDP 3-45.1, 2007; *Green Book*, 2010). Facilities are explicitly designed to reinforce the key messages of the campaign and as such focus on events or visits that will reiterate these themes. They often coincide with newsworthy incidents, particularly visits from senior government officials, or are used as a means of countering adverse coverage elsewhere. Media facilities are also considered to offer particularly good opportunities for the military to engage with journalists, and convey key messages through visual media such as television and photography.[3]

Thirdly, the military also provide embedding opportunities. 'Embeds' are accredited war correspondents who are attached to or accompany a military front-line unit to enable reporting from the 'front line'. Accreditation is granted at the discretion of the MoD. Accredited correspondents are subject to security vetting and required to operate under the terms of operational security. As a result, their copy or broadcast footage is vetted in order that they do not publish or divulge operationally sensitive information. They are also subject to military orders and training (*Green Book*, 2010). Embeds have to provide their own communications and transmission equipment and are encouraged to wear distinguishing 'media' insignia when working with units in the field.

The working arrangements under which the military operate with the media during conflict and peacekeeping missions are outlined in a document known as the '*Green Book*'.[4] According to the military, these arrangements are broadly agreed between the military and media agencies and predominantly cover the practical arrangements for the media to report on events in the United Kingdom and in a theater of operations. The *Green Book* was originally drafted in 1982 after the Falklands War and was more recently updated to accommodate new working practices and terminology.[5] The *Green Book* provides details of registration and accreditation procedures, the regulation of accredited correspondents, including security vetting and embargo procedures, the facilities made available for accredited and non-accredited correspondents and the constraints of reporting on casualties and prisoners of war. In addition, the Joint Doctrine and Concepts Centre (JDCC) in the MoD have produced a Joint Warfare Publication (3-45) entitled 'Media Operations', the purpose of which is to provide guidance for commanders and staff involved in Media Operations. It includes information about the philosophy and context of Media Operations as well as mechanisms needed for the planning and execution of Media Operations. Through the provision of all these facilities, at both a strategic and tactical level, Media Operations work is fundamentally organized around the need to attain support among diverse national, global and local audiences in line with Information Strategy directives.

In sum, according to military doctrine, Media Operations are a line of military activity that aim to provide information for the media with the purpose of informing the public about operational activities. Such assertions, and the structures in which they sit (described in this chapter) offer a particular view of Media Operations from a military perspective. They should not be taken at face value, but are nonetheless important to the reader's appreciation of Media Operations, providing a foundation of understanding on which this book's subsequent interrogations of military work are based. In the forthcoming chapters Media Operations work is analyzed in accordance with what, why and how the military are attempting to inform the public, both through and with the media, and the bearing this has on the conduct of war.

3   The aims of Media Operations

This chapter considers in more detail *what* the military are attempting to achieve through Media Operations work and *how* it is organized in relation to the environment in which it is conducted. To this end, the discussion first centers on the extent to which Media Operations can be understood as both a form of influencing activity *and* a public relations exercise. In making this distinction the multiple, and at times incongruent, objectives of Media Operations work are made more evident. The second half of the chapter is dedicated to assessing how the military actually organize Media Operations work, particularly around identified contingencies that they believe may threaten the stability and security of the military institution and its operations. In so doing, the discussion highlights how contingencies not only become critical to the formation of action, but how they are also indicative of the degree to which the military conceive of the 'war and media environment' in which they are working as essentially *external* to their own institution.

Media Operations as influencing activity

As has already been indicated, Media Operations are executed in accordance with the aims and objectives of the government-led Information Strategy. Another arm of this strategy, supposedly distinct from Media Operations, is Information Operations, which is organized around attempts to destroy the enemy's 'will to fight' in the battle space:

> Victory is rarely achieved purely through the destruction of an adversary's materiel; the key is to destroy an adversary's Will to fight. Info Ops is the primary means by which Will and the ability to impose Will and exercise command is attacked.
>
> (JWP 3-80, 2002: 1-3)

The main tool of Information Operations is 'Influence Activity',[1] which attempts to influence the adversary's perceptions of their own actions (for example, by undermining both the legitimacy of their leadership or eroding their moral power base) *and* influencing the perceptions of civilians. Using their own media, the military try to promote particular themes and messages that 'seek to persuade, convince, deter, disrupt, compel or coerce audiences to take a particular course of action, or to assist, encourage and reassure those that are following a particular course of action' (JWP 3-80, 2002: 2-3). By communicating messages of moral and physical support to those who oppose the adversary, the military believe that they can potentially 'affect' the battle space, enhancing opportunities to advance their own cause. Within these aims, Information Operations can use deception to achieve an information-based objective.

In contrast to Media Operations, which disseminate information through the global media, information distributed with an Information Operations aim is editorially controlled, precisely selected and distributed through political- or military-owned media, including leaflets or military-owned radio stations like Oksigen (Bosnia), Commando Solo (Iraq) and Rana FM (Afghanistan) (JWP 3-80, 2002: 2A-1; see also Maltby, 2010).[2] Despite this, the military acknowledge that there is potential overlap in Information Operations and Media Operations activities where strategic Media Operations information can have a decisive impact upon tactical Information Operations information-based activities and vice versa, particularly if the media unwittingly collapse the two in reportage (JWP 3-80, 2002: 2-6; see also Badsey, 2001). Consequently, they state that Media Operations must be closely co-coordinated with Information Operations activities: 'Media Ops and Info Ops staff must have clear visibility of each other's plans and operations to generate synergy' (JWP 3-45, 2002: 1-2). At the same time, it is also emphasized that Information Operations and Media Operations actions must remain distinct. Any convergence of the two would undermine Media Operations claims to be honest and truthful in the information provision, and may lead to the impression that the media are being manipulated, deceived or used for misinformation purposes (JDP 3-45.1, 2007: 1-3; JWP 3-80, 2002: 2-5). The ways in which this differentiation is maintained in practice, however, remains unclear both in written doctrine, and among military personnel.[3] As a result, military members highlight that tensions and difficulties can arise in the execution of Information Operations and Media Operations as 'distinct' activities.[4]

More importantly, however, the potential convergence of Media Operations and Information Operations is reflective of a shift in political and military thinking over the last decade toward the increasing importance of 'influencing activities' at both a strategic and tactical level (JDP 3-40, 2009; see also Taverner, 2007). Indeed, some military members now argue that the distinction between Media Operations and Information Operations is redundant because, in reality, influencing activity 'pervades everything we do'.[5] This has been more formally recognized in the development of 'influencing' policies in doctrine since 2009, and the substantial increase in influencing activities in Iraq and Afghanistan.[6] This is important, because while distinctions are made between Media Operations and Information Operations, including the ways in which they are organized and executed, both are fundamentally oriented toward an intent to inform, persuade and influence those who become recipients of the information distributed. The intent and intended recipient of the persuasive communication are thus of central importance. Without intent or an intended audience to persuade, the persuasive message has no relevance. In doctrine, the intent is articulated as the 'End' – that is, the end-state that the communication is attempting to initiate (see JDP 3-45.1, 2007: v). Media Operations and Information Operations are the 'ways' in which this intent is enacted, that is, the ways the 'End' is achieved. To take this analogy further, as indeed it is in doctrine, the media are the communicative 'means' through which the intent (or 'End') can be realized. It is through the media that information is disseminated in a manner that will potentially reach the intended audience. Thus, for the military, the media are the 'key enabler' in the promulgation of themes and messages and the shaping of opinion (JDP 3-45.1, 2007).

In this way, military influencing activity is dependent on the media for its central functions. Like other forms of political communication, it can be characterized as involving a tripartite configuration of the military (as political actor), the media, and those citizens with whom the military are attempting to communicate (see Negrine and Stanyer, 2007). Within this tripartite configuration, however, the power of the media is such that the military must acknowledge and negotiate the rules, aims and production logics of the media if they are to successfully secure the effective communication of their intended messages (see Altheide and Snow, 1979). In this sense, the rationalization of persuasion in military 'influencing activities' is akin to other forms of political communication that increasingly submit to media logic to appeal to the general predispositions of intended audiences and increase the likelihood of their communications being disseminated through the media (Mazzoleni, 2008a, 2008b; Mazzoleni and Schulz, 1999). To this end, and by virtue of their reliance on the media as a 'key enabler', the military must too orient their political persuasive communications to the media in order to harness the potential influence that can be gained from it.

It is undoubtedly for these reasons that positive, even-handed, open and truth-oriented media relations are considered by the military to be essential to successful Media Operations (JDP 3-45.1, 2007). As Aristotle so famously argued, credibility and trustworthiness are the bedrock of effective persuasion. Insufficient regard for the truth, and the obvious positioning of the communicators' interests above those they serve can undermine this. Consequently, and with specific regard to the differentiation in influencing activities, Information Operations and Media Operations must be characterized as distinct, not because they necessarily are but because in doing so the military avoid the impression that they are manipulating the media. This is not to suggest that the differentiation of Information Operations and Media Operations is divisive; although there is blurring in the practice of these two 'influencing activities', they have different intents and intended recipients. Information Operations are focused on the tactical use of persuasion to progress a campaign in the battle space. Media Operations are oriented toward generating political and public support for operations through the endorsement of strategic political objectives under which a military campaign is managed. But, reliant on the media as a means by which to achieve this support, the credibility of the military as an information source becomes imperative to the persuasiveness of the information provided.

With this in mind, Media Operations can be seen as another arm of political persuasion necessary for the conduct of a war campaign. Of course, there is nothing particularly new in this assertion. Numerous analyses have recognized that the media play a constitutive role in forming key channels of communication between political actors and their publics in the enactment of war. Indeed, this is the dominant perspective offered by scholars who engage with the topic of military media management. In these analyses, military media management becomes framed in traditional Clausewitzian terms, motivated by state interests as a 'continuation of politics by other means' (Clausewitz, 1997: originally published 1832). This is important, for it allows us to consider the overarching political intent (and content) of Media Operations work. At the same time, such formulations tend to negate the role of the military as communicative agents in their own right. Instead, the relationship between militaries and states is collapsed, and military media management articulated as simply a continuation of politics through communications, rather than a communicative act involving relatively autonomous military decision-making. Consequently, the degree to which militaries may constitute an independent organization, motivated by their own internal goals and politics, is unobserved. A different view – although not incongruous with the one above – is that Media Operations are actually organized around relatively autonomous military decision-making for the benefit of the military institution and its operations, as much as the wider political aims of the campaign. This does not preclude the notion that Media Operations are politically driven, but rather positions the organization of Media Operations work as motivated by various factors, only one of which is political.

Media Operations as public relations

Although politically directed, the British military is also an institution with its own goals, rules, culture, identity and working practices. This is reflected throughout the institution and is key to understanding how, in considering themselves as independent institution, they need to generate political and public support for their own activities independent of their political governance. As a result, the way Media Operations work as conceived of by military members is often akin to public relations work; that is, strategic communications between an organization and its publics intended to acquire and preserve public support (Vasquez and Taylor, 2000). But, the public relations work of Media Operations is more than merely obtaining and sustaining 'good relations' with one's publics. Rather, the intent or 'Ends' of Media Operations for the military (aside from the political persuasion outlined above) is to gain political and public support to fulfill their own goals *and* safeguard their future (Hall, 1972). Moreover, the ways the military formulate the organization of Media Operations work is symptomatic of how this work is perceived by them to be a necessary adaptation to the environment in which they operate. Thus, the public relations framework helps us to understand the relationship between the organization – in this case the military – and the environment in which they are attempting to sustain their own, independent existence (Waeraas, 2009).

Viewed in this way – as indeed the military do – the organizational structure of Media Operations is founded upon principles of rationality and is contingent on three functionalist imperatives: (1) goal attainment; (2) adaptation to the external environment; and (3) the maintenance of necessary motivation among actors (Lawrence and Lorsch, 1967; Parsons, 1959; Burrell and Morgan, 1979). The ways in which this is articulated by the military is key to understanding how they interpret and give meaning to their own actions and the actions of others – including their political governors and the media – in the organization of their Media Operations work. The following discussion should therefore be read as both an indication of those factors the military consider salient to the organization of Media Operations, *and* a precursor to the next chapter, which interrogates these same factors from a symbolic interactionist perspective.

The continuation of the military institution is founded upon the attainment of three fundamental goals. These are expressed discursively by individual military members, and through the internal cultural practices of the British military institution. They are:

1   to protect and maintain the British military organization now and in the future in terms of securing resources, recruitment and retention;
2   to achieve operational success in terms of attaining operational aims and protecting operational security;
3   to protect British military organization members, including relatives of those members, particularly in terms of sustaining morale and a will to work.

These broad goals constitute the main aims of the British military as a collective institution. They do not entirely reflect the goals of wider political governance, but instead signify what the military consider to be essential to the continued success of their own organization. They ultimately underpin decisions about organizational action and act as a framework for the development of more fluid, subsidiary goals relevant to specific operational aims, including Media Operations. These Media Operations goals are particularly explicit in doctrine and the training of service personnel and in no order of priority can be summarized as (JDP 3-45.1, 2007):

• to gain and maintain domestic political support for military activity;
• to gain and maintain public support for military activity;
• to retain 'freedom of maneuver' from political intervention;
• to maintain internal morale;
• to protect operational security, including protecting British military organization members;
• to gain and maintain alliance cohesion during an operation;
• to counter enemy information campaigns.

Media Operations goals are distillations of fundamental goals and indicate the 'intent' or 'Ends' of Media Operations work while also embodying the challenge that the media are considered to present to both operations and the military institution. From these goals, perhaps the most significant is the attainment of political support in order to protect the future of the military organization in terms of resources of independence. Political support, however, is believed to be partly contingent on the perceived support of the electorate who will obtain most, if not all of their information about military activities from the media. Hence, for the military, popular support translates into political support, which in turn translates into military independence and security: 'Public support enhances the armed forces' freedom of action ... a positive image of military operations supports the wider case for resources' (JWP 3-45, 2001: 1-4; see also JDP 3-45.1, 2007: 1-4). Consequently, a fundamental aim of Media Operations work is to secure positive coverage of military activities as a means of influencing those who are influential in government-thinking, such as politicians, statesmen and political advisers: 'The impact of general public opinion on political decision making should never be underestimated' (JDP 3-45.1, 2007: 2-1). Similarly, public support and political support also permit independence through another 'End'; that is, maintaining freedom of maneuver and avoiding political intervention.

Political intervention in military matters can manifest itself in a number of ways, including restrictions on the rules of engagement, type and numbers of weapons used, numbers of troops deployed or the involvement of political leaders in tactical-level decisions, often against the judgment of military tacticians.[7] The latter is referred to colloquially as the 'long screwdriver' and particularly resented by the military not just because it compromises their independence, but also because it is considered to negate the importance of the specialist military knowledge required to make tactical decisions (see Jackson, 2007).[8] Moreover, some military members suggest that in extreme cases it can undermine the security of an operation or increase risks to military personnel.[9] While some level of political intervention is regarded as inevitable, it tends to be correlated with adverse media coverage of military activity that creates a political imperative to intervene.[10] Positive media coverage that builds and sustains public and political support is therefore seen as a means through which freedom of maneuver can be enhanced and vulnerability to political interference reduced.

Lastly, and at the core of what the military consider to be essential to the continued success of both operations and the organization, is the maintenance of morale. Morale is a significant element of military work and is integral to the achievement of fundamental goals. It is considered the third, but possibly most important, dimension of fighting power; the first component being doctrine and the second physical capability. In simple terms, morale is seen as the deciding factor in a military member's willingness to engage in fighting:

> No doctrine, plan or formula for conducting warfare is likely to succeed without the maintenance of morale.... High morale is characterized by

steadfastness, courage, confidence and sustained hope. It is especially mani-
fested as staying power and resolve, the will to win and prevail in spite of
provocation and adversity.

(JDP 0-01, 2008: 2-3)

Morale is considered essential to secure the will of each individual to deliver
what is required in the battle space. For this reason, the military argue that their
colleagues need to believe, at both an individual and collective level, that what
they are doing is positive, worthwhile and supported by the public: 'Positive
media coverage of deployed military operations sustains morale' (JWP 3-45,
2001: 1-5; see also JDP 3-45.1, 2007: 1-4). Unfavorable media coverage is seen
to significantly undermine this, particularly if it is believed to reflect the public
mood. Reports about military casualties are seen as especially distressing and
demoralizing, not least because there is concern that they will also generate
anxiety among relatives and friends 'back home'. Consequently, securing positive coverage of military activities to maintain morale becomes an integral Media
Operations goal. It not only helps to protect military members, but also becomes
a means through which the military can achieve their fundamental goals.

What becomes evident in the articulation of these goals is that their attainment is contingent on the gaining and maintaining of public support for operations and the military institution. In this sense, public relations work is central to
the practice and organization of Media Operations. It is through public relations
that the military attempt to communicate and build relationships with their
publics. However, as stated earlier, it is more than simply maintaining a 'good
image'. If the ultimate aim is to achieve goals to protect the continued existence
of the organization, then Media Operations are in fact an attempt to legitimate
what the military do for the benefit of their institution. As Metzler (2001: 321)
observes, 'establishing and maintaining organizational legitimacy is at the core
of most, if not all, public relations activities'. It is through this legitimacy that
the military institution is able to acquire the right to exist in its current or desired
form, and to conduct operations in the manner that best suits the military's own
needs. Yet, drawing on Weber's notion of 'domination', Waeraas (2007) argues
that legitimacy is not something that can be claimed through public relations
work. Rather, legitimacy is socially constructed and only achievable through the
continued endorsement and support of citizens who perceive an organization to
be worthy of legitimation. Ultimately, then, the survival of the military institution becomes predicated on their ability to strategically influence public opinion
toward believing that the military organization, and its operations, are legitimate
and worthy. In turn, this allows us to see that Media Operations goals are, in
fact, legitimation goals that reflect the degree to which the military see themselves – and their relations with their publics, both internal and external – as
independent from political governance. Thus, unlike the influencing described
above as political persuasion, this influencing activity is oriented toward the protection of the military institution rather than advancing political aspects of war
that the military may be involved in. This is important because it helps explain

why and how the military manage Media Operations in a manner so as to protect themselves.

Moreover, as Waeraas (2007) contends, organizational existence is a privilege that must be justified through public relations, particularly when the organization faces criticism or is under attack from its various publics. If we apply this thinking to current military Media Operations, we can see that attempts to promote 'widespread understanding' are the means through which they can justify and cultivate perceptions of their work as legitimate. Notably, this is being enacted against a backdrop of long-standing and historical criticism with regards to both their actions and media management. This has been well documented and there is no benefit from rehearsing it here other than to say that it is with this criticism in mind that the military currently organize Media Operations in the ways they do.

In particular, great importance is placed upon the need to be proactive: 'Media Operations emphasize the benefits of a positive and proactive approach rather than a defensive and reactive one' (JDP 3-45.1, 2007: 1-3). This is characteristic of the shift in military thinking from a position of hostile censorship to one of public relations in recent years (Dandeker, 2000; Taylor, 2000; Badsey, 1994). Cognizant that defensive and reactive Media Operations have not worked to their advantage in the past, the military thus attempt to proactively engage the media in their activities. In so doing, they attempt to place themselves in a better position from which to 'set the media agenda' rather than having to defend their position at a later stage. In this sense, implicit within their emphasis on proactive approaches is a defensive orientation to their work with media.

Media Operations as responsive

While Media Operations goals indicate the intent of Media Operations, they do not indicate *how* Media Operations work is organized to realize political and military 'Ends'. This is more comprehensible and tangible as what Perrow (1961) labels operative goals. Operative goals illustrate the procedural aims and specific content of *how* Media Operations goals may be achieved, regardless of what the goals are stated to be. They are therefore procedurally oriented and consist of what the military actually aim to do in Media Operations work, rather than what they want to achieve. Moreover, they make apparent the ways in which the military conceive of the environment in which they operate as one that they must continually respond and adapt to if they are to be successful. Operative goals are particularly explicit in the training of service personnel and Media Operations doctrine, and including the following (see JWP 3-45, 2001; JDP 3-45.1, 2007):

1   to harmonize and coordinate all Media Operations information with the Information Strategy;
2   to be open, truthful and factual within the realms of operational security;
3   to actively and positively engage with the media;

4   to meet the needs of the media in order to gain maximum coverage;
5   to treat all media even-handedly and retain credibility with the media;
6   to educate the media regarding military matters;
7   to develop rebuttal procedures to counter the effects of inaccurate or unbalanced media stories.

Although fluid, these operative goals form the basis on which decisions regarding Media Operations will be judged. In particular, they demonstrate the degree to which proactive engagement with the media is seen as significant to their achievement of Media Operations goals. Thus, meeting the needs of the media is the means through which the military can achieve Media Operations 'Ends' by defining military action on their own terms for wider dissemination. Similarly, treating all media even-handedly, being open and truthful and positively engaging with the media are all means through which they believe they can build relationships with journalists that are credible. Through this credibility may come trust in the definitions they are presenting and therefore a greater potential for coverage to be favorable to military terms and the meeting of Media Operations goals.

In addition, operative goals also reflect how the military take account of perceived contingencies that threaten the stability and security of the military institution through Media Operations work. These contingencies are critical to the formation of action in Media Operations work and are indicative of how the military perceive the media environment in which they are working as *external* to them in the sense that contingencies are not generated by the military but instead by the media environment in which the military operate. Consequently, Media Operations are organized around efforts to preempt or respond to particular contingencies which are believed to be produced by the media. One such contingency is the speed of media communications and decision-making. This is argued to exert particular pressures on Media Operations endeavors not just because of technological advances that permit coverage of events as they unfold, but also because of the structural patterns of communication in media institutions that often allow media decisions to take effect immediately. Articulated through a nuclear weaponry analogy of 'flash to bang',[11] – describing the time interval between an event and its response – the military argue that the media 'flash to bang' is an 'unrelenting 24 hour activity' (JDP 3-45.1, 2007: 1-5). The challenges that this generates to Media Operations work are seen as enhanced by the demands of tight media deadlines and the media's short-term focus, which offers journalists little time to reflect upon or analyze the events they are reporting (JDP 3-45.1, 2007). Indeed, the military argue that it is the ubiquity of the media and its unrelenting 'flash to bang' that can, in part, be blamed for the blurring of strategic, operational and tactical actions: 'Through the media spotlight, minor tactical events can escalate to have strategic effect and generate a need for strategic leaders, such as government ministers, to respond quickly' (JDP 3-45.1, 2007: 1-4). Consequently, when the military state that they must harmonize and coordinate all media operations information with the Information Strategy, it is with reference to these contingencies.

Coupled with this demanding 'media spotlight', the commercial culture of journalism is perceived to engender competition among journalists, increasing the constant demand for newsworthy information where 'accuracy can be traded for speed and exclusivity' particularly among certain media organizations (JDP 3-45.1, 2007: 3-1). If devoid of information to report, the military argue that journalists engage in speculation or predictive reporting in an attempt to make sense of what might be happening or to be first with the news (JWP 3-45, 2001: 1A-1). As Shibutani (1966: 164) argues, if the demand for news exceeds the supply made available through formal channels, then rumor construction is likely to occur as those involved attempt to construct a meaningful interpretation by pooling their collective intellectual resources. In an effort to preempt or respond to this contingency – what the military term the 'information vacuum' – Media Operations are organized around the need to generate a constant flow of positive newsworthy material to meet the media's need for stories and images (JWP 3-45, 2001: 1A-2; JDP 3-45.1, 2007: 3-2). Similarly, and related, the perceived need to educate the media on military matters is argued to be necessary to avoid inaccurate or superficial reporting of military activities. The military suggest that journalists tend to lack the relevant knowledge of military affairs with which to interpret events. For the military, the resulting media coverage has the potential to significantly undermine operational security and the safety of military members (JDP 3-45.1, 2007). In addition, they argue that inaccurate reporting creates pressure for them to explain events without due process, thereby opening opportunities for the further delivery of inaccurate information. In turn, this makes them vulnerable to accusations of disseminating falsehoods if information supplied to journalists subsequently transpires to be wrong.[12] Hence, in an attempt to preempt, or respond to these contingencies, the military believe that it is in their interests to educate journalists on military matters (such as equipment and operational planning) in order to secure coverage that, in their terms, is more likely to accurately represent their activities.

All of these contingencies highlight the kinds of challenges the British military believe the media environment presents. In the formulation of their procedural processes and operative goals the military take account of these contingencies in an attempt to preempt or protect against their occurrence. The dominant understanding of Media Operations among the majority of military personnel is therefore one of a purposive system geared to the fulfillment of goals. The structure is considered to be an expression of, and determined by, organizational adaptation to objective and identifiable environmental contingencies. Most importantly, these contingencies are understood as being external to the military institution in the sense that they are not generated by the military, but instead by the media environment in which the military operate. Although this view may be shifting, alternative perspectives fail to be expressed with clarity or consistency, discursively and in military doctrine. Thus, for most of those working within Media Operations, the 'environment' is external, objective, identifiable, and something that *happens to* the organization, rather than something of which *it is part*. This is particularly evident in the ways in which the military discursively formulate *how* they will attempt to achieve Media Operations goals, which indicate elements of a more traditional, protective orientation toward working with the media. In particular, the language used in the planning of Media Operations is often defensive, suggesting a continued reticence toward dealing with the media, despite their reliance on them.

On the one hand, then, Media Operations seeks to harness the power of the media as a means by which to politically persuade and influence audiences within the overall strategic objectives of both the military and the political framework in which the military institution sits. To this end, the military adapt their behaviors to the logic of the media because the media is instrumental to their realization of political persuasion and military goals. Proactive Media Operations are indicative of this, and also highlight the degree to which Media Operations are shaped by interactions between the military and the media. Concurrently, however, and perhaps because of the degree of scrutiny that the military institution has and continues to come under as a result of the media's watchdog role, a traditional reticence toward military media engagement remains. This is important, because while the military appear to be constructing an image of transparency and 'openness', there will continue to be occasions when they guard against or attempt to prevent media observation of their activities.

4 Media Operations

An interactionist perspective

In the previous chapter the organization of Media Operations was shown to be purposive, goal-oriented and perceived, by the military, as continually adapting to contingencies produced within the 'external' media environment. In marked contrast to this view, this chapter proposes that Media Operations both shape and are shaped by the interactions that take place between the military and the media. To this end, Media Operations are considered to be a military 'performance' in accordance with Goffman's (1959) notion of impression management. This performance is intended to influence the impressions that others come to formulate of military activities and as such is organized according to the ways in which the military interpret and give meaning to their own actions and the actions of others. This provides the starting point for subsequent analysis, which is committed to developing a conceptual toolkit through which we can better understand how Media Operations are performed, and the implications of such performances for the conduct of modern military operations.

Media Operations are the primary means through which the military can define their activities for media audiences at a political, domestic and global level. The impressions that audiences form are considered critical to meeting the aims of the Information Strategy while also contributing to acquisition of legitimation and preservation of the military institution. It is through the generation of favorable impressions that the military believe they will be able to attain military goals, particularly in terms of securing resources, retention, recruitment, sustaining internal morale and the will to work. Media Operations are therefore, fundamentally, a form of impression management work.

Situated within Goffman's notion of the 'interaction order', impression management is the act of managing one's identity during social interactions in a manner that attempts to influence and control the conduct of others:

> This control is achieved largely by influencing the definition of the situation which others come to formulate, and he can influence this definition by expressing himself in such a way as to give them the kind of impression that will lead them to act voluntarily in accordance with his own plan.
>
> (Goffman, 1959: 15)

Here we return to the importance of influence. For Goffman, this influence is achieved through the presentation and performance of a public self. Drawing on a drama metaphor, Goffman (1959) compares face-to-face interaction between individuals to parts played by actors in front of audiences. In the presence of others, an individual not only attempts to acquire information about others, but also constructs a 'front' through their own performance in order to generate impressions favorable to the performer that will exert influence. In this drama-turgical analysis, Goffman terms the place where this performance is acted out as the 'front region' or 'front stage' where expressive equipment, such as appear-ance, setting and manner are used to define the situation for those who observe it (1959: 109). In contrast, the 'back region' or 'backstage' is where the perform-ance is constructed and fabricated, where impressions are openly contradicted and where others have restricted access (1959: 114). It is in the back region that the performer can 'relax; he can drop his front, forego speaking his lines, and step out of character' (1959: 115).

While focused on interpersonal interaction, Goffman's concepts of perform-ance and impression management have significant utility in illuminating our understanding of organizational and political persuasive communications *and* the building of relations with external publics where the establishment of trust and confidence are important components (Johansson, 2009). Essentially, organ-izations, like individuals, are 'actors' engaging in 'performances' before 'audi-ences' (Allen and Caillouet, 1994).

Predicated on the ability to achieve influence, either as political persuasion or a legitimation exercise, Media Operations can therefore be seen as impression man-agement, performed in interaction with media organizations in an attempt to influ-ence the impressions that others will come to formulate regarding military activities. All of these performances are concerned with coherently and collec-tively defining military activities for the media in a manner that will encourage or persuade audiences to act in accordance with military objectives and institutional goals. An integral component of this work is to guide the actions of the media in order to secure the communication of military definitions to intended recipients.

For this reason, and because the military classify their audiences as members of the public rather than members of the media, a literal application of Goff-man's notion of impression management to Media Operations has some limita-tion, because its analytical understanding of performance derives from direct, co-present interaction between performer and audience. In contrast, Media Operations work is predicated on a mediated relationship with the audience, enacted through the media, and in which the media have a translating and inter-pretative role. Further, as Meyrowitz (1985) points out, the front and back regions of Goffman's dramaturgical analysis – where the performance and con-struction of definitions take place, respectively – are often tied to physical loca-tions, limiting our understanding of social interaction through the media. This point is particularly pertinent to impression management performances of Media Operations, which are rarely determined by physical setting but rather by the degree to which the military believe their activities will be visible for public scrutiny. To this end, Meyrowitz's concept of the 'information system' is useful in its ability to offer a framework of analysis for military impression management through and with the media. For Meyrowitz, the 'information system' comprises patterns of access to social information about the actions of others. He defines social information as '[a]ll that people are capable of knowing about the behavior and actions of themselves and others ... access to each other's social performances' (1985: 37). The information system is not therefore limited to face-to-face encounters, although it can include them. Instead, it is a more inclusive concept through which people acquire information about others, involving impression management both in and beyond those interactions that occur in place-bound settings.

By employing the concept of the 'information system' here, both co-present and non-co-present forms of military impression management work can be explored. In this sense, Media Operations impression management should be understood as a determinant of information flows, rather than place-bound settings. Moreover, the information system also allows us to conceptualize what the military consider to be the 'ubiquity' of the media and its impact upon their performances. As stated previously, when the military highlight the ubiquity of the media they are generally referring to the amplified distribution of information about their activities as a result of competitive global media outlets. For the military, this phenomenon has led to an increasing media demand for new information about, and unique insight into, operational activities beyond that which is provided in Media Operations. Due to advances in media technologies such as lightweight camera equipment, improved communication speeds and real-time technology, the military acknowledge that journalists are now able to obtain a diverse array of information about tactical events that undermine an otherwise reliance on official military definitions. All of these factors can be understood in terms of increased patterns of access to information about military activity in the information system. Such increased patterns of access are critical to how the military organize impression management performances.

Impression management and the institutional self

With this in mind, Media Operations performances can be seen as a collective team performance of impression management, in which military members collaborate to project and sustain definitions of military activity. In this sense, these performances are a form of 'joint action' in which individual military participants fit their lines of action to one another (Blumer, 1969: 70; Goffman, 1959: 85). However, while comprising separate lines of action, Media Operations performances are distinctive in their own right and do not need to be broken down into separate acts in order to ascertain their meaning. Instead, the meaning lies in how the military, as an institution, formulates and organizes performances in response to how they define and interpret Media Operations situations. In this sense, 'institution' is taken to mean a common response on the part of all members of a community to a particular situation, where the distinctive character of joint actions and the interlinkage of separate acts can be identified without reference to their constituent separate lines of action (Mead, 1967: 260; see also Blumer, 1969: 17). For the British military, the meaning of perform-ances is ascertainable through their articulation of goals, which are expressive of how and why Media Operations are considered important to both an operation and the organization. Operative goals, in particular, reflect the ways in which the military interpret and attribute meaning to their own actions, and the actions of others, in order to direct and guide their impression management performances. In this sense, operative goals can be used to explain the outcome of this interpre-tive process, for it is with them in mind that the military organize their perform-ances in particular ways in interaction with the media.

The process by which the military are able to interpret and give meaning to their impression management performances in relation to the actions of others is possible by virtue of their possessing an 'institutional self'. The concept of the 'institutional self' draws upon Blumer's (1969) and Mead's (1967) 'sense of self', which is developed when an individual becomes an object of their action. It is used here to describe how the military, in the organization of their perform-ances, become an object of their own action, placing themselves in the position of others and viewing themselves from that perspective in order to direct their own action. As a result of being an object of their action, the military interrogate their own actions, and those of others, in order to evaluate how best to organize Media Operations in line with the activities of the media. This is evident in the common responses among military members regarding how they are, or will be, perceived by others if they adopt a particular course of action. For example, they believe that if they are slow in providing information to journalists, they will come to be perceived as reticent and obstructive.

It is through these attempts to understand their own actions from the perspec-tives of others that the military have recognized that it is in their interests to appreciate, rather than rally against, the information-gathering needs of the media in order to achieve the effective communication of their own definitions. And, it is here especially that a military interrogation of their own previous actions is critical to the formation and organization of current performances (see Blumer, 1969: 20). They argue, for instance, that the historical lack of impor-tance dedicated to media management – evident in the allocation of minimal resources and a culture of antagonism toward media demands for information – has been instrumental in the generation of impressions of the military as uncoop-erative and secretive. In turn, this has subsequently undermined their attempts to secure the communication of military definitions in media reportage. In response, they now attempt to orient their performances and interaction with the media toward proactive, rapid and open engagement in order to avoid the generation of suspicion and mistrust among journalists. This is indicative of the military's pos-session of an 'institutional self' with which they interrogate their own behavior, and from which they formulate Media Operations actions.

In addition to viewing themselves from the perspective of others, the military also take account of the actions of others and the impact this may have on their own actions. Hence, when military members argue that the structure and organization of Media Operations have developed to their current forms in response to the contingencies produced in the media environment, they are implicitly identifying how they organize Media Operations actions in accordance with the actions of others. By considering what others are doing, or are about to do, they direct their own behavior in accordance with what they take into account (Blumer, 1962). This is evident in the development and organization of operative goals that take account of the potential contingencies generated by the actions of others and the impact this may have on the attainment of military goals. For example, the education of journalists about military matters is organized on the basis of their taking into account the perceived potential for journalists lacking in specialist knowledge to produce distorted or superficial reportage. The provision of educating facilities is also directed by the potential for 'distorted' coverage to generate a decline in public support, which in turn can give rise to a number of other contingencies such as a lack of political support, political intervention or weakening of morale. Hence, when taking account of the actions of others, the military are also assessing the likely consequences of these actions on the future of their operations and organization. Consequently, they modify their organizational procedures and actions in an attempt to guide others' actions in a manner that will lead to the generation of favorable impressions, avoid contingencies and ultimately advance the achievement of goals.

When the military take account of others' real and anticipated actions, they are engaging in what Goffman terms 'properties of play' by considering the likely consequence of their actions for others; others' likely response to that consequence; and the bearing of that response on the military's own future actions (Goffman, 1969: 47; see also Mead, 1967). The military, then, organize their actions on the basis of these assumptions, incorporating that which they calculate will usefully influence others' responses. Again, this is reflected in the articulation of operative goals, which are formulated in accordance with how the military believe they can best influence the responses of others. It is through these operative goals, and the formulation of actions with which to achieve them, that the fundamental goals of the institution may be realized. Without the joint actions arising from operative goals, the military are less equipped to influence the responses and actions of others in the Media Operations environment.

Shaping the environment: the military contribution

In their interaction with the media, the military contribute to how others organize their own actions in two key ways: first, through their proactive defining of situations in a manner that attempts to generate favorable impressions; and second, through their management of anticipated contingencies that threaten to bring about unfavorable coverage. Both of these processes are indicative of how, in contrast to the military view, Media Operations are not merely organized reactively – that is, in *response* to the actions of others or identified contingencies – but are in fact organized proactively in an effort to guide and control the impressions that others will have of them. In this sense, the 'Media Operations environment' is not external to the military institution, but rather comprises the actions of all those involved in the reportage of operational activity, including the military. This point is critical to understanding how all parties involved organize their actions in accordance with the real and anticipated actions of others, which cumulatively shape and are shaped by Media Operations work.

Let us first consider the proactive defining of situations. In their attempts to generate favorable impressions, Media Operations are organized so as to define military activities for the media in order that they are communicated to audiences. Knowing that this requires proactive engagement with the media, the military have developed doctrine, procedures and facilities oriented toward meeting the needs of journalists. It is through these structures and actions that the military contribute to the construction of the Media Operations environment by initiating the means through which journalists can report. Through the organization of performance opportunities, such as press information centers and media facilities, the military attempt to guide and direct the actions of journalists in their reportage of military activities. These provisions define the conditions and terms on which the military and the media will engage during operations and are designed by the military in a manner that they believe will assist them with the achievement of their own goals. Similarly, the registration and accreditation of journalists, while argued by the military to be a procedural means through which they accommodate and protect journalists,[1] also enable the military to limit the number and status of those journalists with whom they will be required to interact. In this way, the organization of Media Operations is instrumental to the formation of how, when and where the military will interact with the media during operations. For, while the military organize their actions in accordance with their taking into account the actions of others in the environment, journalists also direct their own behavior in accordance with how they interpret and give meaning to military performances. By constructing specific reporting opportunities, the military essentially 'set the stage' not only for their own performances, but also for the other actors involved in the setting.

The second way in which the military contribute to the environment is through their anticipation of, and attempts to manage, potential contingencies. In their assessment of the Media Operations environment they not only take account of the real actions of others, they also take account of the potential or anticipated actions of others and use this information to orient their actions. This is clearly illustrated in the military's identification of contingencies, and the organization of their own actions in response, and in a manner they believe may prevent such contingencies occurring. Again, the education of journalists is a particularly good example of this process. In effect, they attempt to counter another's action prior to it occurring, rather than responding to it when it does occur. Goffman terms these 'tacit actions', in which one adapts one's actions to another's response before it has been called forth, in such a manner that it never has to be made (Goffman, 1969: 47). Hence, in contrast to the dominant military view, Media Operations not only comprises responsive actions, determined by the real actions of others in the environment, but also includes proactive actions based on the military's orientation to the anticipated actions of others. It is through their use of tacit actions in particular that the military contribute to the shaping of the Media Operations environment.

The utility of a Goffmanesque approach to understanding Media Operations work helps elucidate the degree to which military media management is in fact a product of social relations between military and media agents. This is apparent in the military engagement in 'properties of play' and the consequent organization of Media Operations to incorporate that which will usefully influence others and assist with the attainment of goals. An integral component of this work is to attempt to guide the actions of the media in order to secure the communication of military definitions. Media Operations thus become a product of interactions and social relations that must be constantly attended to if the military 'front' is to remain intact or enhanced for organizational gain (see also Brown and Levinson, 1987). It is within this theoretical framework of impression management that Media Operations are described and explained throughout the remainder of this book in order to interrogate how the military define their activities and the implications of their performances for ongoing war operations.

5   Audiences

Imagining and influencing

So far, this book has been concerned with the degree to which Media Operations is predicated on the military's desire to achieve influence, either as political persuasion or a legitimation exercise. Drawing on Goffman's (1959) dramaturgical perspective, it has been suggested that Media Operations is actually a form of impression management performed in interaction with media organizations in an attempt to influence the definition others will come to formulate of military activities. All of these performances are concerned with coherently, and collectively, defining military activities for the media in a manner that will encourage or persuade audiences to act in accordance with military objectives and organizational goals. Before considering how the military construct definitions of their activities, it is first necessary to explore in more depth with whom they are trying to communicate and for what 'Ends'. This chapter is thus concerned with describing the ways in which the military construct their sense of audience. To this end, an important analytical distinction is made between military 'audiences' as the intended recipients of military definitions, and 'media observers' as communicators of military definitions – for it is with audiences in mind that the military formulate definitions of the situations from which impressions will be formed and influence achieved. The following discussion is intended to show why the military aim to generate particular responses among particular audience groups. It provides the foundation for the subsequent analysis regarding *how* the military attempt to achieve these aims through Media Operations impression management work.

Audience groups

As a result of possessing an 'institutional self' and being an object of their own action, the military are able to assess the Media Operations environment and use the information available to them to try to respond effectively to what is happening and what is likely to occur. Simultaneously, they appreciate that others within the environment, such as the media and audiences – including the adversary and the political and diplomatic community – are engaged in the same process. Hence, they are aware that it is in their interests to control and manage the types of information that others might obtain about their activities in order that they can influence others' responses in their favor (Goffman, 1969; Mead, 1967). In order to do this effectively, the military must conceive of a sense of audience for whom definitions are constructed, and among whom impressions and responses will be manifest. The military are able to identify their audience(s) by engaging in 'properties of play', whereby they consider the likely responses to their definitions by others in the environment, and the bearing of that response on the military's own future actions (Goffman, 1969: 47; see also Mead, 1967: 154). Those whose responses have a significant impact on the strategic and tactical activities of the military organization are thereby identified as the audience for whom definitions are constructed.

Devoid of a context in which to carry out impression management in direct interaction with the audience, the military classify their Media Operations audience as members of the public, rather than members of the media. This analytical distinction between the public 'audience' and media 'observers' is critical to a conceptual understanding of how the military define their activities. While definitions must accommodate the information-gathering needs of the media, it is primarily with audiences in mind, rather than media observers, that definitions are constructed. As stated earlier, the media are seen as the 'key enabler' in the promulgation of themes and messages to the 'intended recipients': 'The primary purpose of Media Operations is to communicate information to an audience. In this sense, the media are only a means to an end' (JWP 3-45, 2001: 1-5; see also JDP 3-45.1, 2007: v). Consequently, the media are conceptualized here as 'observers' in accordance with Goffman's notion of strategic information management where a subject – in this case the military – attempts to influence in their favor the definitions that observers come to form of their activity (1969: 10). While the term 'observer' may suggest a tendency toward passivity, it is used here to make explicit the distinction between the media and the military's audiences. Indeed, the following chapters demonstrate the degree to which media observers are in fact active in their engagement with the military. For now, it is relevant to make the distinction between those who observe definitions of military activity as the media and those who receive these definitions through media coverage as the audience, in order to explore what kind of responses the military are attempting to draw forth from their Media Operations work.

At the same time, given the distanciated relationship that the military have with their audience, and the potentially vast and heterogeneous composition of this audience group, it is inherently difficult for them to ascertain and generalize, with any certainty, who their audiences actually are and what their potential responses may be. Instead, they construct a sense of their audiences, based upon the limited information available (see also Espinosa, 1982; Pekurny, 1982; Gill, 1993). This construct is essentially an 'imagined audience' among whom particular responses to impressions are desired. While the actual responses of the imagined audience are difficult to gauge with any accuracy, the potential for responses is critical to the formulation of military impression management performances. When taking into consideration the potential responses of the others, the military take the role of the imagined audiences to interrogate their actions from the point of view of those audience groups in order to gauge how their actions may be perceived and understood. This can be understood in accordance with Mead's notion of the 'Generalized Other', in which performers take the role of others:

> Each of his [the performer's] own acts is determined by his assumption of the action of the others who are playing the game. What he does is controlled by his being everyone else on the team, at least so far as those attitudes affect his own particular response. We get then an 'other' which is the organization of the attitudes of those involved in the same processes.
>
> (Mead, 1967: 154)

Essentially, then, the audience or audiences, as the 'generalized other', comprise those whose attitudes, beliefs and potential responses determine military impression management. To this end, the military classify their audiences into three key groups: the external audience, the internal audience and the adversary audience (JWP 3-45, 2001; JDP 3-45.1, 2007). Within each of these three groups there are various sub-groups whose differentiation is analytically important to an appreciation of how, in the construction of definitions, the military attempt to communicate specific messages simultaneously to multiple audiences.

The external audience

The external audience represents wider public opinion and consists of the political audience, the home audience, the coalition audience and the civilian population in the theater of operations. The primary sub-group in the external audience is the 'political audience'. Essentially, these are key decision-makers in the national and international community or those whose opinions may be highly influential on the direction of government or alliance thinking and policy development. They include members of parliament, political advisors, defense analysts and academics. The principal target audience in the external category, however, comprises the domestic UK 'home audience' – the UK public – who are further broken down into sub-categories of media allegiance, ethnic and religious groups and the business community. Differentiation between these groups is understood in terms of how their situated position may inform their impressions of the armed forces.

The support of the 'home audience' is of particular importance to military operations for the two key reasons stated earlier. First, their support is considered crucial to maintaining continued political support for both the long-term future of the organization in terms of resources, and short-term success of an operation in terms of avoiding political intervention. For the military, political support is perceived to be partly contingent on the support of the electorate, who will obtain most, if not all of their information from the media. As such, fostering favorable impressions of their activities among the 'home audience' is a means of obtaining political support.

Second, their support is also considered critical to the maintenance of internal morale. Military members need to believe that the UK public is supportive of military activities, believing them to be worthwhile and valuable. Without this, the military argue, morale and the will to work can be directly undermined, thereby threatening operational success and the long-term retention of troops.

Lastly, the external audience also includes the domestic audience associated with coalition countries and allied partners. Given that operations are rarely conducted unilaterally, the British military are usually one of a number of coalition partners involved in a war campaign. Favorable impressions resulting from media coverage are seen as critical: 'Success may well depend on continuing political support among "friendly" audiences abroad.... Indeed, it is usually the case that the strategic centre of gravity for such operations is the cohesion of the alliance and coalition' (JDP 3-45.1, 2002: 2-2). Generating an image of a united coalition 'front' is key in this regard, not only to the success of the campaign itself in terms of sustaining coalition cohesion, but also to the public and political support generated among wider international audiences who witness coalition activities via media reportage.

The internal audience

The internal audience is comprised of those with some affiliation to the military organization – more specifically, those directly and indirectly involved in the conduct of an operation. The internal audience consists of two major groups: (1) military personnel and (2) the families of service personnel, otherwise known as 'dependents'. Aware that military service personnel have access to the media on deployed operations via television, the internet, radio and second-hand from their own kin, Media Operations work takes into account the military audience in the same manner as other audiences:

> On operations, many Service personnel become avid news watchers/listeners, tuning in to Satellite TV, BBC World Service and the Internet. Much of their knowledge of the wider operation in which they are involved develops from the information put across by the general media, rather than through the chain of command.
>
> (JWP 3-45, 2001: IB-1)

The military believe that impressions of operations gained through the media may have a significant impact upon morale and the will to work among service personnel, particularly if they are negative. Impressions formed among the friends and families of service personnel are of similar importance for similar reasons, particularly because families will tend to be more knowledgeable about and affected by operational events than non-related UK audiences:

> Families are a key audience for Media Operations. They have a direct effect on the morale of the deployed force. While the chain of command will

attempt to keep dependents fully involved, the reality is that TV news and the print media are a major source of information for many Service families.

(JDP 3-45.1, 2001: 2-2)

These impressions also have the potential to directly affect the morale of a deployed force if families communicate them back to service personnel in theater via letters or phone calls.[1] Further, there are concerns that impressions generated may also affect subsequent recruitment and retention (JWP 3-45, 2001: 23). For these reasons, dependents become a key target audience for Media Operations, for it is through the generation of favorable impressions among them that the military attempt to protect the security of both the operation and the organization.

The adversary audience

The adversary audience is identified as adversary service personnel, the government of the adversary, their leadership and the adversary's allies, who are variously categorized as supporters through treaties, ethnic and religious groups and shared values (JWP 3-45, 2001; JDP 3-45.1, 2001). This audience group may also include the civilian population in a theater of operations who might support adversary activities. The media is considered to present particular opportunities to communicate with or directly address this audience group, not least because the military perceive it as a means through which to counter 'enemy propaganda'. It is with this audience in mind, however, that the overlap of Information Operations and Media Operations becomes more tangible. Essentially, they are the primary audience for Information Operations, which, through military-owned media, attempt to influence the adversary and 'their' local civilian population. Thus, in broad doctrinal terms the external and internal audience is the focus for Media Operations work, while the adversary audience is the primarily focus of Information Operations. Yet, cognizant that adversary audience groups can access global media in the battle space, strategic information emanating from Media Operations work is seen to have a decisive impact upon tactical Information Operations work and vice versa. Consequently, definitions of military activity in Media Operations work are also constructed with this audience in mind.

Generating audience responses: belief and action

While these audience groups are analytically distinct, at the level of generated impressions they are interrelated. Impressions formed in one group can affect the impressions formed in another. If, for example the political audience perceive the impressions among the home audience to be unfavorable, it creates a greater imperative to intervene in military matters in order to maintain the political support of the electorate. Similarly, if the internal audience perceives the impressions among the political audience or home audience to be unfavorable, there is a greater likelihood that internal morale will decline. In this sense, while Media

Operations definitions are designed to communicate specific messages to specific audience groups, attempts are made to coordinate definitions so as to generate favorable impressions across all audience groups.

Given that the aim of Media Operations is to generate audience responses in accordance with military goals, the military need to identify what types of responses they are attempting to elicit in order to know how to define their activities in order to draw these responses forth. This is key to how media definitions come to be constructed. As indicated earlier, the essential response required from *all* audience groups is support for military activities. This represents the macro-level at which the military aim to generate responses. At a more micro-level, the desired response may vary according to the category of audience (i.e. political audience, home audience, dependents or the adversary). Hence, while definitions may aim to generate support and non-intervention among the political audience, the same definitions may be purposefully constructed to bring about fear and capitulation among the adversary audience, or to boost morale and the will to work among the internal audience. Media Operations are therefore concerned with defining military activities in particular ways to engender specific actions among specific audience groups. Consequently, there are two levels at which Media Operations definitions attempt to generate responses. These are conceptualized here as 'belief' and 'action'.

'Belief' is a concept used here to explain what the military empirically refer to as 'support', discursively categorized as 'public support'. Yet, the term 'support' implies an act of expression on behalf of the audience, which, given the distanciated relationship between the military and their audiences, is inherently difficult to determine. The information flows between the military and audience are essentially uni-directional, and patterns of access to information about audiences are restricted. Hence, the degree to which audience support is measurable as a response to military impression management is limited unless it is manifest in a demonstrable act such as letters, phone calls, a public demonstration or political critique. When, therefore, the military use the term 'support', what they are implicitly referring to is a *belief* that widespread support exists across audience groups as a result of impressions generated through Media Operations work. This 'belief in support' is devoid of any active quality and is essentially unmeasurable. With the exception of some external audience polling undertaken by the Foreign and Commonwealth Office, the military have few means through which to measure the actual impact of media coverage on audiences. Instead, in the absence of tangible data regarding audience responses, the military tend to correlate Media Operations success – that is, bringing forth desired responses – with media coverage that includes or reinforces Media Operations themes and messages.[2] For this reason, a significant amount of time is dedicated to the monitoring and analysis of media coverage both in the MoD and in the Media Operations center in the theater of operations. This analysis focuses upon evaluating existing media 'stories' and anticipating and predicting future media coverage. From this, 'threads' emerge – the term used to describe what the story is and where it might be going – and decisions made regarding how the military can best manage any 'thread' concerns.[3] As such, when the military express concerns about 'threads', what they are actually doing is expressing concerns about the perceived impact these threads may have on audience responses. In turn, this is based on the assumption that media coverage is a reflection of audience feeling and response.

Of course, in reality this process circumnavigates how audiences actually perceive, interpret and understand media reportage of military activity. Instead, success is measured by a 'good story'.[4] Not only does this assume a uniform response among audiences, but also assumes that this uniform response will be one of support if the coverage is favorable. This is reminiscent of the hypodermic needle model of media influence – so evident in initial evaluations of the Vietnam War – in which audiences are seen to uniformly and passively respond to media stimuli (Kraus and Davis, 1976; Carruthers, 2000). Ultimately, because military definitions are constructed in such a manner as to create positive and sympathetic impressions of the military, their successful mediation thereby becomes associated with a belief in widespread audience 'support'. What results, however, is a solipsistic relationship between what the military are doing and how they attribute meaning to what the media are saying they are doing. In this way the military are further 'imagining' their audiences based on perceived responses they believe will be forthcoming, which in turn are based on indicators constructed from the media coverage itself. The simplicity of these formulations fails to account for the complex and dynamic interaction between media content, audiences and their interpretive frameworks. Consequently, audience responses to media coverage of military activity are, in reality, elusive. As Berelson *et al.* (1954: 356) point out: 'Some kinds of communication, on some kinds of issues, brought to the attention of some kinds of people under some kinds of conditions, have some kinds of effects.' For the military, however, it is the perception that media coverage reflects the public mood, and thus audience responses, that leads them to focus almost entirely on the coverage itself (see also Molotch *et al.*, 1987). This is important because it highlights the degree to which the military believe they are interacting with their audiences through and with the media, making them further reliant on the media as a communicative tool. In turn, this also highlights the degree to which audiences – and their potential responses, whether real or not – influence the organization of military action. Indeed, this becomes more evident in the second level of desired response: *action*.

Action is when audiences 'act' in response to military definitions in accordance with military objectives. Unlike 'support', *action* is measurable in that it involves an expression of an act, restricted to specific audience sub-groups. Actions can be palpable in behaviors such as the non-intervention of political agents, an increase in internal morale or, at an organizational level, an increase in resources or upsurge in recruitment. Of course, these actions may occur separately from Media Operations impression management work, not least because some audience members have a distinct and direct relationship with the military organization that is neither mediated nor operation specific, such as political governors or dependents of military members. Moreover, these actions may derive from other tactical military activities, such as Information Operations. It is therefore difficult to ascertain the correlation between actions and Media Operations definitions with any accuracy. Despite this, the manifestation of these actions is nonetheless associated with the impressions that audiences *might* form as a result of Media Operations work. Once again, it is the potential that media coverage could be influential in generating action that leads the military to associate media coverage of their activities with audience responses.

Crucially, as implied in previous discussions in this book, attempts to generate actions in response to Media Operations definitions are understood to be contingent on the existence of *belief.* This is because the military believe that audience members will take account of the information available to others, and the potential responses of others, in the formulation of their own actions. In this sense, audiences are also considered to be engaging in the same 'properties of play' in which the military engage to formulate their own actions. For example, the military understand political non-intervention to be founded on the belief among the political audience that other audience groups – especially the UK home audience – are supportive of military actions. Similarly, morale and a will to work among military members is seen as contingent on a positive, supportive response of the political and public audience. Essentially, for the military, audiences are understood to be more likely to consider embarking on certain actions if, in their assessment of the environment, they too consider there to be widespread belief (or non-belief) in military activities.

Media Operations impression management work is therefore fundamentally concerned with constructing definitions of military activities that will generate *belief.* By endeavoring to generate belief, the military increase the chances of provoking secondary *actions* particular to each audience group. The need to generate belief is universal to all operations and organizational activities. Similarly, while some actions vary according to the specificity of an operation, the majority of actions are also largely generic to all operations. Among these generic actions, some are desired for their strategic effect in terms of maintaining alliance cohesion, inducing support among all audience groups and protecting the future of the military organization. Other actions are desired for the effect they will have at a tactical level, such as the avoidance of political intervention in operational decision-making or the sustaining of morale among troops. All of these responses can be grouped in accordance with the audience among whom the military wish to generate the desired action (see Table 5.1).

To further clarify this with an example, we can compare the British military deployment to Sierra Leone in 1999 – executed under United Nations Resolutions to aid the local Sierra Leone government in quelling violent uprisings by the Revolutionary United Front (RUF) – and those during the Iraq War and the war in Afghanistan. Desired responses across all these campaigns were generically similar at both a strategic and tactical level.

Although the political frameworks in which these operations were conducted were quite different, each intervention was argued – politically and militarily – to be predicated on the *necessary* provision of frameworks for peaceful and

Table 5.1 Desired responses at the level of belief and action

Audience	Definitions	Examples of desired actions	Desired effect strategic or tactical
Political	Operation is worthy and well executed. Intolerance of instability in particular regions, including those beyond the theatre of operations.	Retain 'Freedom of Maneuver'. Non-intervention in tactical military decision-making. Allocation of resources for military activities at operational and organizational level.	Tactical and strategic
Home	British government and military embarking on decisive action in an unstable region. Operation is worthy and well executed.	Potential future recruitment. No direct action but belief in support from home audience translates into action among other audience groups.	Strategic
Civilian population in theater	Operation will provide framework for peace and democratic governance.	Active involvement and cooperation in military tactical activity such as provision of intelligence information or rising up against adversary in alliance with military forces.	Tactical
Military personnel	Operation is valuable, supported and worthy of involvement.	Sustained or increased morale. Sustained or increased will to work. Retention of military personnel at organization level.	Tactical and strategic
Dependents	Operation is valuable and worthy of each soldier's involvement.	Increase in morale among both dependents and military personnel. Retention of military personnel at organizational level.	Tactical and strategic
Adversary	Operation is supported internationally, well resourced and well executed.	Decrease in morale and will to work in adversary troops. Decrease in active support among allies of adversary. Capitulation of adversary.	Tactical and strategic

democratic governance in the countries concerned, and from which they would benefit. Media Operations definitions of military activities were constructed on the basis of these political aims, and in turn the impact this would have on the military organization. For instance, the success of all these operations is partly contingent on the cooperation of internal military personnel and the civilian population in theater, alongside sufficient resources and support among the public, political and diplomatic community.

At a generic level, then, Media Operations definitions are constructed to achieve these aims by stressing the robustness and physical capability of military involvement in situations that are worthy of military intervention. At a tactical level, this is believed to translate into messages of reassurance for populations based within the theater of operations, a message of 'we are here to help you and have the power to do so'.[5] This was certainly the case initially in Iraq and Afghanistan, although the shift toward counterinsurgency activities in both of these operations served – to some degree – to undermine these messages and instead highlight the military's potential impotency in the face of guerilla attacks and civil disruption.[6]

In Sierra Leone, messages of reassurance became critical to tactical implementation of the operation and as a means through which the military could mobilize the local civilian population to assist with the quashing of rebel forces.[7] At a wider strategic level, Media Operations definitions are also used to dissuade allied countries from contributing to the destabilization – or continued destabilization – of the theater of operation through political alliance or resource allocation. For example, in Sierra Leone the military wanted to dissuade Liberia from backing the RUF (the rebel forces). Similarly, in Iraq and Afghanistan attempts to maintain good political and diplomatic alliances were considered crucial to dissuading surrounding countries (such as Iran and Pakistan) from contributing to further destabilization and threatening military operations.[8] The audience groups with whom they are attempting to communicate, and the strategic and tactical actions that the military desire in response to these definitions, are thus generically similar.

Despite this generality, however, definitions are clearly differentiable in their detailed content relevant to the context of each particular operation. Indeed, the military claim that they were particularly successful in their dissemination of, and generation of responses to, definitions of military activity in Sierra Leone as a direct result of the operation's specific context. As a 'peace keeping' operation executed under the legal framework of the United Nations, Sierra Leone was easily definable as an intervention executed to instill peace and stability in a region rather than an aggressive campaign. Further, media interest existed prior to and during the military deployment, focusing in particular upon the heightening instability of the country and RUF human rights violations. The military argued that this existent media coverage, primarily focused on human suffering and rebel atrocities, especially the severing of hands to prevent locals from election voting, enabled them to construct positive definitions of their own activities as 'liberators' and 'good guys' with relative ease.[9] In a sense, the media had already defined the situation for them in a manner that was distinctly to their advantage.

In contrast, the military argue that the Iraq War presented significant challenges for their Media Operations work from the outset. First, the existence of initial support for military intervention was questionable, particularly among the UK public and wider international community. This created an environment in which the military found themselves competing with information in the media that ran contrary to their attempts to define the war as 'justified' and 'worthy'.

Second, in the absence of UN backing, political and military definitions stressing the value and legitimacy of the campaign were also undermined. Because of this, it became difficult for the military to define their involvement in simplistic 'good guys vs. bad guys' terms as were used in Sierra Leone. Moreover, the progression toward counterinsurgency and the apparent inability of the military to combat insurgent activities effectively – certainly in the initial instance – continued to undermine Media Operations efforts to define the British military role as one of maintaining security and re-building Iraq.[10] Similar problems were encountered in Afghanistan, where the motives for – and legitimacy of – the campaign were continually called into question. Despite these evolving factors, however, in the initial stages of each of these campaigns Media Operations work was fundamentally oriented toward attempting to project particular definitions of the military as a liberating rather than aggressive force.[11] It is with this in mind that the next chapter considers the particular techniques used to try and achieve these aims.

For now, it is important to note that through Media Operations the military define their activities in a particular manner in order to encourage or persuade audiences to act in accordance with military organizational and operational goals. The multiple 'imagined' audiences for whom the military construct definitions are those whose responses to impressions are considered to have a strategic and tactical effect on military work. By attempting to influence the impressions that these imagined audiences come to form, Media Operations definitions aim to generate *belief* among all audience groups, and particular actions among particular audience groups. For the military, the existence of belief tends to be correlated to the successful mediation of military definitions over other competing definitions. Predicated on this is *action*, which is the manifestation of specific behaviors among specific audience groups. While the detailed content of definitions can be operation-specific, the generation of belief is universal to all operations and organizational work. Drawing on empirical data from military operations, particularly from the Iraq and Afghanistan wars, the following chapters consider in more detail *how* the military define their activities in a manner that attempts to secure their effective communication by media observers, while also appealing to all the multiple imagined audiences to generate this belief and action.

6   Defining war
Control moves

This chapter is centrally concerned with exploring how the military construct definitions of their activities. Of course, in reality, defining is not separate from but is rather intrinsically linked to performance in impression management. But, for the purposes of clarity, the forthcoming chapters impose an artificial distinction between the 'defining of situations' and the 'performance' of Media Operations. Hence, Chapters 6 and 7 are analytically oriented toward assessing how the military proactively and reactively explain and account for their activities through 'definitions'. Chapters 8 and 9 then focus on how the military attempt to secure the communication of these definitions through the performative aspects of their impression management. In this vein, the focus of this chapter is to interrogate the content and form of Media Operations definitions to elucidate how they are designed to appeal to multiple audiences while simultaneously meeting the information-gathering needs of the media. To this end, definitions are analyzed in accordance with Goffman's (1969) notions of 'control moves' in that they are intentionally and self-consciously produced by the military to enhance their situation. The degree to which the military are limited in their capacity to achieve these aims, and the ways in which they attempt to manage resulting discreditable situations is explored in Chapter 7. For now, this chapter aims to highlight why and how the military submit to the logic of the media in the construction of their definitions.

Linguistic, visual and narrative control moves

Media Operations definitions are the means through which the military attempt to control what is *revealed* about their operational work. To this end, the construction of definitions about military activity is informed by three key aims, which form the basis on which Media Operations definitions are discussed in the remainder of this chapter:

1   Definitions must incorporate and reinforce the strategic and tactical aims of the Information Strategy in order to be effective in drawing forth responses among multiple audiences and maintain a cohesive 'front' for the operation.

2   Definitions must appropriately meet the information-gathering needs of media observers in order to secure their effective communication.
3   Definitions must be protected from disruption if they are to be effective in drawing forth the desired responses among multiple audiences.

In order to assess how best to construct definitions, the military try to perceive them from the point of view of each audience group *and* media observers. As a result, they believe that definitions need to be broad in their content to simultaneously appeal to multiple audiences. At the same time, these same definitions must be attractive to media observers so as to ensure their communication through the media. Through linguistic, visual and narrative defining strategies the military thus explain, account for and demonstrate action in a manner that attempts to achieve these ends. This can be understood in accordance with what Goffman terms 'control moves', which he defines as:

> an intentional effort by the subject to produce expressions that he thinks will improve his situation if gleaned by the observer.... They are self conscious and calculated. The subject appreciates that this environment will create an impression on the observer and attempts to set the stage beforehand.
>
> (Goffman, 1969: 11)

In the same manner that individuals utilize speech and symbolic body language as means of expression, the military similarly construct definitions of their activities through linguistic, visual and narrative control moves. It is through the content of control moves that the military convey key themes and messages from which they hope to elicit responses among audiences. Their form, however, is consciously designed to meet the demands of the media and therefore pre-prepared and stage-managed in line with what the military understand to be the media's requirements. This is imperative if the military are to enhance the possibility of securing the communication of the definition. Concurrently, the form of the control move, including the grammar and style is also oriented toward the audience and the interpretative frameworks – or logic – they will employ to assess and understand the mediated definition. This aspect of form is less obvious and self-conscious in military articulations of definition construction but nonetheless apparent in the ways they design definitions for easy interpretation. Essentially, in the organization of the definition material (language, image, etc.) the military attempt to explain potentially complex situations in accessible and appealing ways in order that the audience will comprehend and respond in a manner from which the military will benefit. Through the combined content and form of control moves we can not only see what the military are trying to say, but how they are trying to say it in a manner that submits to the logic of the media. Again, in the analysis of military definitions it is difficult to differentiate the content from the form of control moves. One often informs the other. Despite this, the remainder of this chapter attempts to first explain *what* the military are attempting to communicate through linguistic, visual and narrative control moves, before moving on to interrogate *how* they try to secure the communication of these definitions through specific strategies and techniques that are aligned to media needs.

Linguistic control moves

Linguistic control moves are understood here as those that utilize language to convey particular themes and messages in definitions of military activity. These themes tend to be broad and similar across most campaigns and are usually devised in accordance with the strategic aims of the Information Strategy and thus emanate from the joint political efforts of all those nations involved in the campaign. Because they are coalition-generated, they are fundamentally tied to the notion of the 'team performance' as they act as a means through which each participating nation attempts to persuade audiences of coalition alliance and cohesion. Essentially, these definitions provide a branded 'front' under which each nation's Media Operations work operates and comprise generic but enduring concepts in order to be communicable across diverse populations. Moreover, they employ positive, emancipatory terms to define military activities as liberation exercises rather than invasions,[1] such as: 'Towards Freedom', 'Iraq for Iraqis', and 'Force for Good'.[2] They are intentionally designed to be non-specific, but to include and reaffirm common moral values that fit the expectations of the groups to whom they are presented. In this sense, they correspond with Goffman's (1959: 44) notion of the 'idealized' performance in that they incorporate and exemplify the accredited values of society, although often more so than the actual behavior as a whole. 'Idealized' military definitions therefore stress concepts like freedom, democracy, protection and justice on the assumption that they will appeal to audiences across the political, commercial and domestic spectrum and across diverse political, religious and ethnic groups.

Beyond the wider strategic directives of these definitions, similar concepts and terminology are used to define military action in a manner that has both strategic and tactical intent. Phrases like 'the will to prevail' and 'overwhelming power'[3] are thus used to define the military as a committed and technologically powerful force. Definitions such as these have multiple purposes. At a strategic level they are trying to generate support among the external audience; at a tactical level, they attempt to weaken the morale of the adversary, and simultaneously reassure civilians in the battle space that the military are committed to their emancipation. This was certainly the case during the operations in Sierra Leone and Iraq. In fact, the timing of these definitions in the months leading up to the start of the Iraq War was considered to be of critical importance to the strategic success of the campaign.[4] At this time, and in competition with unfavorable media coverage, these phrases were designed to provide an overarching framework under which it was hoped the war would eventually come to be understood once operations began in earnest. Consequently, they formed the foundation for all subsequent political and military definitions throughout major combat operations (which ended in April 2003) and were perceived to be successful in this regard.

Despite the perceived success of the above definitions in relation to the Iraq War, the military acknowledge that there are occasions when definitions fail in their global appeal precisely because they are not 'idealized' enough. Examples they cite include President Bush's use of the term 'crusade' in reference to operations in Afghanistan, which was interpreted by some (although the military do not specify who) as a 'war against Islam'. Also cited was the Pentagon's use of 'Operation Infinite Justice', used in response to the attacks of 9/11 to 'brand' operations in Afghanistan, but later renamed 'Operation Enduring Freedom' because of perceived negative religious connotations.[5] Similarly, the focus on the headscarf as a sign of the oppression of women in relation to definitions of Afghanistan was retrospectively acknowledged as detrimental to the strategic campaign, although predominantly because the definition itself was seen to be 'misinterpreted'[6] rather than naïve or prejudiced in its assertions about Islamic culture. In some respects, this suggests a rather solipsistic orientation to political and military rhetoric, and latent ethnocentricity in the conception of what is idealized.

Common to all of these slogans, themes and definitions is that they seek legitimation through the setting up of binary oppositions: freedom vs. restriction, good vs. evil, etc. This is important, for perhaps the most significant of these is the construction of the adversary as a threat in opposition to military claims that promise safety. Indeed, most of the conceptual phrases utilized in military definitions are accompanied by assertions regarding an existing threat to the country relevant to the operation, and often to wider global security. Certainly this was the case with the Iraq and Afghanistan wars, where it was claimed that weapons of mass destruction (WMD) and terrorism, respectively, constituted a direct threat to the United Kingdom. As a classic rhetorical device, this construction of binary oppositions enables political and military actors to ground their practices and the struggles of war in metaphorical and mythical representations of good vs. evil, safety vs. threat. These representations are not only accessible and meaningful to audiences, they also serve as an anxiety-reducing mechanism. Essentially, by creating anxiety and fear among audiences, these definitions simultaneously seek support and legitimation for a military operation by constructing it as a solution to the 'threat'. The effectiveness of these oppositions is even greater if fear of the threat already exists. Under these conditions, definitions attempt to attach to and elicit feelings around the existent fear in a manner that justifies the proposed military 'solution' (see also Diamond and Bates, 1984). In this sense, phrases that utilize concepts like 'liberation', 'freedom' and 'justice' are more than simple assertions. Rather, they are part of a wider project of dichotomy construction from which the legitimacy of the operation is proffered and sought.

Visual control moves

Further to the ways in which the military define their activities linguistically, and in the knowledge that images can 'brand' an operation, the military also attempt to define their activities visually: 'In terms of grabbing attention and helping shape perceptions, a picture can be a defining image' (JDP 3-45.1, 2007: 3-2). In this way, they construct image-based definitions for the media that can purportedly be taken as they appear. The incorporation of visual definitions into Media Operations work has a dual purpose. First, pictures can convey particular definitions in a manner that linguistic phrases are unable to do because they are not language-specific. As Bryan Whitman, US Assistant Secretary of Defense stated of imagery in the Iraq campaign, 'Images are important. They are even more important in certain parts of the world where language can be a barrier' (*Correspondent: War Spin*, BBC 2, 18 May 2003). Second, visual imagery is considered important to both the communication of specific messages, and the reinforcement of conceptually based linguistic phrases and explanations.

For these reasons, visual control moves tend to be based around two key aspects of military work which are also dichotomized in their focus on the opposing aspects of military work: aggressive vs. reconstructive. The visuals associated with aggressive military work, and through which the military attempt to reinforce definitions of technological superiority power, are 'kinetic' images (firepower, military machinery, and so on). Thus, for the military, the images of the coalition bombing of Baghdad during the Iraq War dramatically symbolized coalition airpower and commitment to the Iraq campaign, reinforcing the existing linguistic definitions of 'the will to prevail' and 'overwhelming power'.[7] The perceived effectiveness of these images was located in their display of coalition technological superiority, which would encourage support among external audiences and capitulation among the Iraqi forces.[8] In opposition to these 'aggressive' images are those focused on the reconstructive, stabilization and humanitarian aspects of military work, through which 'liberating' definitions can be reinforced. To this end, after the initial securing of Basra in 2003, the military encouraged the media to capture images of troops substituting helmets for berets, organizing football matches with local civilians and distributing humanitarian aid.[9] All of these types of actions are considered to have clear strategic benefits if communicated to the external, internal and adversary audiences by defining military action in more progressive and cooperative terms. Essentially, visual control moves are not merely a means through which the military attempt to define particular activities symbolically. They also complement and reinforce broader, strategic linguistic definitions that embrace binary oppositions. As a result, a significant element of defining activity is now oriented toward incorporating a visual component.

Narrative control moves

Lastly, in addition to generic visual and linguistic definitions, the idea of 'narrative' has increasingly come to the fore in the ways in which the military attempt to define their activities. Again, directed by the Information Strategy, the narrative concept is hinged upon the perceived need to support political and military strategy with a 'story'.[10] In accordance with typical story construction, the narrative control move enables operations to be presented as a series of chronological actions; the motivation for the operation (beginning), the intended resolution to the operation (ending) and the actions required to achieve that resolution (middle). The narrative thus becomes the means through which information can be presented to audiences as a connected series of events with a logical structure: from disruption through to the reinstatement of equilibrium.

In these classic Todorovian (1988) terms, narrative becomes a device through which military intervention can be constructed as generating 'transformation' and resolution. Transformation is usually represented by a country's improved stability, governance and security, brought about by military intervention. Again, this was the case with Sierra Leone, where the development of democratic governance was defined as directly related to British military intervention in the quashing of the Revolutionary United Front (RUF). Similarly, transformation in Afghanistan is represented as the development of Afghan governance that can guarantee stability and security, and, crucially prevent a terrorist presence.[11] The logical series of narrative events that will culminate in this 'transformation' of Afghanistan are presented as: (1) the securing and sustaining of security in all Afghan regions; (2) the consolidation of security to introduce governance and economic development; and (3) the handing over of responsibility for security to the Afghan National Security Forces, who can ensure their own security and facilitate improvements in governance and socio-economic development.[12]

Inherent within this narrative, although not as explicit in doctrine, is the threat that the Taliban present to both the stability and security of Afghanistan, and also the security of the United Kingdom. It is in this construction of the Taliban as a threat that we can locate the binary oppositions so essential to the narrative's progression. As an antithesis to the Taliban villain, the military become the hero. This is not a whimsical point. All narratives are reliant on characters whose initiations and responses to others develop the 'story' and drive the narrative forward (Propp, 1968). In this sense, the ways in which the actions of the Taliban – or insurgents – are constructed in the narrative gives us some indication regarding how the military are attempting to define their own relative position. Either insurgent defeat becomes defined as military victory, thereby drawing the narrative closer to its end, or insurgent victory becomes justification for the assessment of the insurgent threat and therefore the presence of coalition forces.

This use of the narrative is a particularly sophisticated communicating tool in wars where 'winning' is difficult to define.[13] In the absence of clear, predictable and bi-polar interpretative frameworks through which the media can explain conflicts like Afghanistan, the 'narrative' and its construction of heroes and villains allows the media to report in simple, accessible terms for the sake of viewers' understanding. Moreover, for the military, and because of the longevity of conflicts like Afghanistan, the narrative allows them to explain the operation as a series of sequential steps toward 'progress'. This is considered necessary if audience belief in the legitimacy of the campaign is to be sustained. Given that operations extending beyond their original timescale (otherwise known as 'mission creep') have long been a political and military concern,[14] the narrative becomes a key means through which potentially unfavorable responses to mission creep can be diffused. Moreover, the narrative control move detracts from the 'winning'/'losing' dichotomy. Instead, chronologic 'transformation' and progress become the central message.

'Define or you will be defined'[15]: strategies and techniques

What all these strategic defining devices have in common – linguistic, visual and narrative – is that they are constructed in accordance with how political and military actors believe audience groups and media observers will perceive them. To this end, they are broad in their content in order to simultaneously appeal to multiple audiences but also, crucially, constructed in a manner that will be attractive to media observers in order to secure their effective communication. In support of these definitions, Media Operations work therefore incorporates specific strategies and techniques with which to fortify these aims.

One of the ways in which this is managed is through 'profiles'. Profiles gauge, identify and categorize the level of media interest in particular issues or activities in order to design appropriate military responses (JDP 3-45.1, 2007). In an 'Active Profile' attempts are made to actively encourage and rouse media interest; in a 'Passive Profile' attempts are made to pacify media interest; during a 'Semi-Active Profile' the military seek to provide information for the media but in a manner that does not intensify this interest (JDP 3-45.1, 2007: 4-2). All of the profiles are indicative of the self-conscious and calculated manner in which the military employ 'control moves' to set the stage in advance of offering definitions. In particular, responses to media queries in both the Passive and Semi-Passive Profiles are fundamentally designed to satisfy media demand for information (so as to not appear obstructive), but only to avoid 'uninformed' speculation, confusion and rumor (JDP 3-45.1, 2007: 4-2). In this sense, all of these profiles are a proactive means through which the military attempt to avoid being reactive at a later stage. The majority of Media Operations definitions, however, sit within an 'Active Profile'.

In an effort to persuade the media – and in turn audiences – that a particular reality exists, the military consciously select and deliver a particular definition in a manner that will reinforce the key themes and messages they wish to convey.

One of the techniques employed to achieve these ends is discursively referred to as the ABC technique: 'Answer, Bridge, Communicate'.[16] Under the umbrella of this technique, military definitions attempt to incorporate (1) a clear articulation of the 'facts' they wish to convey; (2) a 'bridge' to the themes; and (3) communication of the key message. The bridge is also used to assert definitions associated with the military's own goals and therefore will incorporate concepts like 'preparedness', 'professionalism', 'commitment' and 'capability'. The use of the ABC technique is especially apparent in military briefings, statements and interviews with military personnel. For example, in an interview about gas attacks during the Iraq War, the ABC technique was used to (1) stress the threat of gas; (2) bridge to the theme of military professionalism and preparedness; and (3) communicate the key message regarding military capability in the forthcoming operation and thus the likelihood of victory:

> As you said, we have had to respond to a number of alerts over the past 12 hours but actually routine has carried off. One of the things we've been doing since we've been out here is making sure that we can respond if something happened and that has happened this morning and we have responded.... We have spent time training, taking into account all the potential missions required and making sure that we are ready for any of those should that be required.
>
> (Captain Fred Gray, *ITN News*, 20 March 2003)

As indicated in the quote above, techniques like the ABC are considered particularly useful for defining activity in a manner that connects tactical activity with the strategic aims of the overall campaign. Through this connection the broad and overarching concepts of 'liberation', 'emancipation' and 'threat' are evoked. For instance, when interviewed about the discovery and destruction of Iraqi weaponry on the road into Basra in 2003, the ABC technique was used to connect (1) the tactical discovery of 300 mortar rounds with (2) the significance of the find in terms of military achievement and defusing risk, which was then used to (3) segue to claims regarding the threat of the Iraq regime:

> In terms of weaponry there was a find some 300 metres up this road. 300 mortar rounds, some RPG rounds, quite a considerable find. Obviously this represents the threat we face.
>
> (2nd Lieutenant Andy Shand, *Channel 4 News*, 27 March 2003)

It is through this final point that the threat of the adversary, so crucial to the linguistic defining process, is emphasized as a means to strategically justify the operation as legitimate and emancipatory. Similarly, when Iraqi civilians incurred mortar fire while attempting to leave Basra in 2003, in contrast to Iraqi accounts that stated the British had fired upon the civilians, the British military defined it as a Ba'ath Party assault on 'hungry', fleeing civilians (*Channel 4 News*, 28 March 2003). In so doing, the military definition not only accentuated the threat of the Ba'ath Party toward vulnerable Iraqi civilians, but concurrently suggested that the assault was illustrative of the party's loss of power in the region:

Here we see perhaps the initial signs of the Ba'ath Party, the irregular, losing an element of control of their own civilian population who clearly they wish to keep inside the town for their own purposes, and that therefore, while not being over optimistic, is a good sign.... What we are trying to do is eradicate this Ba'ath Party political control that keeps the lid on the people. The irregulars are the architects of that by using force against them.

(Colonel Chris Vernon, *ITV News*, 28 March 2003)

Again, recurrent themes are evident in the prominence given to the adversary's loss of power and the military's 'liberating' role.

Similar messages have emerged in relation to the war in Afghanistan, where insurgent improvised explosive devices (IEDs) or suicide bombings that have maimed and killed are implicitly defined as the actions of the desperate: '... insurgents have resorted to ...'.[17] The deflection of potential military involvement is also evident in reportage regarding the military treatment of Afghan civilian casualties, which tends to focus on the professional and 'caring' nature of military medical practice rather than the circumstances in which they came to be injured (see, in particular, *Ross Kemp in Afghanistan*, Sky One, February 2009). More broadly, the lack of security in Afghanistan and its effect on the civilian population is continually defined in terms of the unpredictable, oppressive and desperate adversary threat rather than a military inability to contain the situation.

To this end, the military define the 'facts' of a situation for their own gain, enhanced by the use of specific 'defining' techniques. ABC is one of them. Lines to Take (LTT)[18] is another. LTT are the constant and consistent reiteration of a definition to assert its validity. Through LTT the military essentially attempt to persuade audiences of a particular reality while often deflecting attention away from other, perhaps more controversial issues.[19] The majority of LTT emanate from MoD 'core scripts', which are formulated in response to anticipated media questions. LTT are carefully managed, and military members briefed in advance so as to avoid being drawn on subjects that may be strategically or tactically damaging. Indeed, at the least sophisticated level, LTT are particularly evident in common, identical responses from military members such as 'We are here to do the job we trained for.' In this sense, both LTT and the core scripts from which they derive are akin to Goffman's (1959: 91) notion of the 'thin party-line', in which the military collaborate to project and sustain a definition of a situation, reducing the reality espoused to one that is both simple and unanimous.

While the impenetrability and repetitiveness of LTT can be frustrating for media observers, they provide a relatively 'safe' technique through which military members, from all levels of the military hierarchy, can define military activity without undue risk to existing definitions. For the military, this is important. It allows them an opportunity to generate an impression of accessibility and transparency (rather than denied access and control), which in turn may help bolster their credibility. Indeed, making military team members available for interview is now seen as critical to the generation of favorable impressions because the military believe that the use of civilian media advisers or media experts would only incur accusations of spin and overt public relations.[20] The military 'face' is thus vital in the presentation of the credible military 'front'. Furthermore, by pushing military members to the fore of Media Operations work, especially Commanders or military spokesmen, the military provide 'characters' with whom the media and their audiences can identify.[21] These 'characters', especially if used repeatedly, not only drive the narrative forward, but also become symbolic of more concrete processes in a manner that detracts from the social and political implications of conflict to which they refer (see also Levi Strauss, 1987; Fiske, 1987). It is through this metonymy that reality comes to be constructed in particular ways, and from which the military stand to gain.

Further to linguistic defining techniques, the military also recognize that providing good imagery, or opportunities for the media to capture good imagery, is a prerequisite for successful media reportage. As stated in doctrine:

> The media seek a visual component to all stories. Dramatic TV footage frequently determines whether a story is given airtime or not. The availability of striking photographs will often determine how and where a newspaper story is covered.
>
> (JWP 3-45, 2001: 1A-2)

This is a view echoed among many scholars, who consider that most events only become newsworthy when they can be visualized in a media-friendly manner, especially in a manner compatible for television (Brauman, 1993; Moeller, 1999). Indeed, despite the proliferation of new media outlets, political actors are still almost wholly dependent on television for mass audience reach (Castells, 2009; Blumler and Kavanagh, 1999; Swanson, 1997). Thus, as a form of persuasive political communication, visual definitions of military activity are increasingly oriented toward meeting the visual needs of the media in an attempt to secure their communication. Moreover, by offering visual opportunities, the military also believe they can avert the media search for alternative, perhaps more speculative information on which to report.[22] Visual imagery is thus as much of an appeasement to media needs as it is a strategy through which to define military work. Chiefly, there are three ways these visual control moves are asserted in Media Operations, aside from the regular press briefings: combat camera teams, media facilities and embedding.

Combat camera teams are military camera teams whose material is disseminated to the media and government departments. Owing to the military's editorial control over the material, they consider combat camera footage to be particularly beneficial to the communication of specific definitions and messages while providing the media with the drama and action they desire for reportage. The advantage for the media is that it provides them with imagery of scenes, places or incidents to which they are otherwise unable to go. Examples from the Iraq War, for instance, include the capturing of Iraqi prisoners of war and night-vision shots of air deployments.[23] As one journalist stated:

Increasingly, there are MoD teams filming stuff, soldiers, who unlike the spokes [journalists] really do get to the front and really do see what's going on and really won't shoot some of the stuff but really will shoot other stuff, they just know without being told. Very interesting, the MoD are very keen on that, there is a big future in all that.

(Channel 4 correspondent, interview data)

For these reasons, combat camera footage has been increasingly incorporated into Media Operations work. However, given that primary authorship is the responsibility of the military, the military are aware that it can challenge the neutrality and independence essential to the media's own legitimacy, and thus stress that better marketing and promotion of such material is essential if it is to be used by the media (JDP 3-45.1, 2007). Consequently, other visually defining opportunities are organized for the media to observe and film military activity in a manner that can purportedly be taken as seen.

Of these, the dominant method is media facilities, which are organized events or visits oriented toward providing media observers with the opportunity to film kinetic or reconstruction activities, not least because it will appeal to the media demand for drama and human interest, respectively. Of these two, the military acknowledge kinetic media facilities tend to be more popular among media observers precisely because they are more dramatic. As one Media Operations staff member explained, media observers particularly favor facilities with tanks or demonstrations by the engineers where they 'blow things up, build bridges and destroy things'.[24] To this end, the military organized numerous media facilities during the 'build-up phase' of the Iraq War, when troops were amassing on the Kuwait border and when the military were trying to assert definitions of their activities in terms of impressive physical manpower and resources through which they could 'liberate' Iraq. In particular, equipment demonstrations, briefings with vast numbers of gathering troops, training sessions and visits to field hospitals were organized.[25] The resulting media reportage suggests that the military were relatively successful in their attempts to secure the communication of these intended messages in the media. The BBC, for instance, stated: 'In the Gulf, there is no doubting the huge potential firepower of the military force building here' (*BBC News*, 20 March 2003).

For the military, this type of coverage is particularly favorable to their impression management aims. Not only might it encourage early capitulation of the adversary, but also strengthen morale among soldiers by virtue of the media attention afforded them.[26]

Kinetic reportage has also emerged from the war in Afghanistan, in both news and documentary form. Increasingly, however, the military are reluctant to encourage this type of coverage. As a counterinsurgency operation, there is little opportunity to assert the technological superiority of the military. On the contrary, 'kinetic' in Afghanistan tends to signify unpredictable insurgent IED explosions, or long, drawn-out firefights that are unpredictable in terms of victory. Under these conditions, media facilities are focused on providing opportunities to reinforce the themes of the sequential narrative of 'transformation' and progress. This was also the case in Iraq after the end of major combat operations, where facilities were organized around reconstruction activities, including mine clearance, humanitarian distribution, and relationship building with civilians (see *BBC News*, *ITN News* and *Channel 4 News*, 1 April 2003). For the military, these facilities symbolically defined the military as trust builders in the progression toward change.[27]

In Afghanistan, evidence of similar progress is critical to the narrative. Visually, this is considered demonstrable against particular topics such as education, governance, security and infrastructure.[28] Thus, media facilities become organized around, for example, visits to schools, Shura meetings or road patrols with both the military and Afghan National Security Force as a means of 'demonstrating' collaboration and progress. The road patrol, in particular, offers opportunities to assert the progress with infrastructure and security: the road has been built, traffic travels on it, people walk on it, there is 'freedom of movement', which in turn implies an increase in security.[29] Organization of media facilities like this may also detract from the ongoing unpredictable kinetic action occurring elsewhere. When kinetic actions do occur, however – such as IED explosions – the military argue that due to a media desire for action and drama the subsequent coverage will almost always focus on kinetic action despite military efforts to avoid it.[30]

Lastly, the military have also come to realize that the ability to effectively demonstrate progress is contingent on comparison. Indeed, recognition of any change demands this; this is how it *was*, compared with this is how it *is now*. For this reason, and especially with reference to ongoing campaigns like Afghanistan, media observers are increasingly being invited, and encouraged, to return to regions that they have previously reported on in order to report again. This is particularly the case with embedded correspondents, who the military believe can offer compelling reportage from a very tactically focused level.

Although subject to vetting for operationally sensitive information, embedding can be particularly advantageous for journalists who are able to witness, and report on, tactical activity as it unfolds. Moreover, there appears to be a lack of military control over communicated definitions, which is reinforced by the apparent unpredictability of the situation that can be reported on with immediacy. As one Channel 4 producer stated with regard to embedding in the Iraq War:

> It was a live war happening right in front of our very eyes and by the public seeing this they suddenly felt this urge, as you do, to support your boys out in the field and they were suddenly behind them and the support for the war went up.... Equally, the gamble was that there would be some dreadful incident and public support would go down, you know its give and take.
>
> (Channel 4 producer, interview data)

From a military perspective, embedding is especially unique in meeting the media need for dramatic and exciting visual imagery while representing a particular reality of battle operations. Indeed, because embedded journalists pre-dominantly shadow – literally and metaphorically – front-line troops, the resulting visual definitions tend to be seen from the soldier's perspective, thereby bolstering the military view. This reportage also appears neutral and objective, devoid of any 'stage management', and so long as the credibility of the journalist remains unchallenged, so does the integrity of their definitions. For the military, embedding also complements other forms of Media Operations work. While press information centers focus on providing strategic definitions, embedding performances can disseminate definitions about tactical activity. Combined, these are considered to offer a comprehensive view of the entire operation. In reality, this failed to happen in both Iraq and Afghanistan as the strategic over-view of the campaign became overshadowed by the often largely uninformative dramatic embed footage. As one critic stated regarding the Iraq War:

> It gave you a real bird's eye view, sometimes very much out of context, sometimes from the point of the battalion but overall without any idea of where they were going, what they were doing or for what purpose.
> (Daniella Pletka, *The War We Never Saw: The True Face of War*, Channel 4, 5 June 2003)

These criticisms are now more readily acknowledged by the military (JDP 3-45.1, 2007). Despite this, embeds are still a key means through which the military attempt to communicate with audience groups. In particular, during the initial stages of the Iraq War, the military considered the increase in public support to be partly attributable to embedded coverage[31] (see also Couldry and Downing, 2004; Lewis and Brookes, 2004). Similarly, the embedding of Ross Kemp with 1 Royal Anglian battalion in Helmand Province, Afghanistan was considered by the military to have been a 'wonderful presentation' of military activity that balanced the risks of embedding with the ability to communicate with the wider public.[32]

Combined, linguistic, visual and narrative control moves are the means through which the military account for and explain their operational activity in a manner that attempts to be generic, idealized and positive in order that they appeal to all audience groups. To this end, they utilize familiar devices inherent in most forms of media-based communication, which will appeal to the percep-tual categories of audiences, but may also enhance the accessibility and inter-pretability of the themes the military wish to convey. Binary oppositions, narrative structures and connotative visuals thus become tools of communication to advance the military cause. Concurrently, this grammar of communication is also suited to meeting the demands of the media to ensure the communication of the definition to mass audiences. Bolstered by specific strategies and techniques, it is here that the military's submission to the logic of the media is most apparent.

7 Defining war
Strategic interaction

Through the coordination of visual, linguistic and narrative 'control moves', the military attempt to define their activities in a manner that will encourage the generation of belief and action. The degree to which the military are limited in their capacity to achieve these aims is explored is this chapter through the lens of Goffman's (1969) strategic interaction and expression games. In particular, there are two factors relevant to the military's inability to achieve the successful communication of definitions. First, in their strategic interaction with media observers the military's reliance on the media as 'communicators' undermines their capacity to define in their own terms. Second, in their use of control moves an environment is created in which media observers will seek to uncover what is being obscured by the military. This subsequently leads to the generation of disrupted or competing definitions that can discredit the military. Ultimately, the environment in which Media Operations take place is shown to result from the actions and strategic interactions of *both* the military and the media, where the interplay of control moves, uncovering moves and competing definitions exist as a product of these social relations.

Drawing upon Goffman's (1969) notion of strategic information management and expression games, the use of control moves is concerned with how subjects and observers – in this case the military and the media – manage information in interaction with each other. Goffman (1969: 10) defines those situations in which both subject and observer engage in strategic information management during co-present interaction as 'expression games'. Here, he argues that while it is in the interests of the observer to acquire information about the subject, it is simultaneously in the interests of the subject to appreciate that this is occurring and to control and manage the information the observer obtains. To this end, the subject turns on himself and looks from the point of view of the observer in order to perceive his own activity from their perspective in order to have control over it. In situations where the observer is dependent on the information provided by the subject – there being no sufficient alternate sources of information – game-like considerations develop and a contest over the assessment occurs. The subject then engages in a sequence of moves, counter-moves and adaptations in an attempt to influence responses to a situation in their favor.

This notion of expression games is utilized here to describe the processes by which the military and media strategically manage information in interaction with each other in an attempt to acquire, reveal and conceal information about their own and others' activities. Such engagement is made relative to an environment that has already been generated by the contest of assessment occurring between the military, their audiences and media observers (Goffman, 1969: 13). The notion of strategic interaction provides a useful framework to interrogate the complex symbiotic relationship between the media and military, in which their respective institutional needs create a dynamic of cooperation and competition, manipulation and resistance. In particular, it offers us a perspective through which we can examine how the military attempt to define their activities in a manner that courts media needs while simultaneously manipulating them for their own gain. Similarly, it allows us to see how the media attempt to glean information from the military from which they stand to gain, while simultaneously trying to expose possible military manipulation relative to their own position. It is here that the contest of assessment is located, which both shapes and is shaped by the interactions of both parties.

Tacit definitions

In order to draw forth intended responses, the military must protect their definitions from what Goffman (1959: 24) terms 'disruptions', which occur when information contradicts, discredits or otherwise throws doubt on the impression the definition is attempting to generate. Protecting definitions requires the military to exercise foresight in their definition construction so they can anticipate the contingencies that may create definitional disruption and prepare responses for these eventualities in advance.[1] In this process of imagining the consequences of their definitions, the military therefore adapt to the possibility of a particular response among media observers in an attempt to prevent its occurrence. Goffman (1969) terms these 'tacit' or 'virtual' moves in expression games in which the course of action – actual or imagined – consists of an assessment and response to that assessment. In a similar manner, the military attempt to anticipate and prepare for specific media-generated definitions that may directly compete with or contradict their own. In their use of tacit definitions, the military are essentially defining a situation in anticipation of media critique before the critique has been made, and in a manner that means it never has to be made (see Goffman, 1969: 47).

The construction of military 'tacit' or preventative definitions is based upon the military's prior experience with the media, but also related to the military's political governance. Because of the perceived interrelatedness of politics and media, military members tend to view their organization as a vehicle through which the politics–media relationship is enacted.[2] Consequently, they argue that they often become a vehicle through which the media attempt to criticize wider governmental and political power. This is particularly evident in their repeated use of the phrase: 'We are a stick with which to beat government.'[3]

The military suggest that, by implication, the media will try to report negatively on their work. In particular, they identify topics that have historically generated media critique and which they anticipate will do so in the future. These include the questioning of a campaign's overall strategy, its timescales, ineffective military equipment, 'friendly fire' incidents and the incurring of casualties.[4] The tactical and strategic effect of these critical media definitions is considered to be especially detrimental to the generation of belief among audience groups. Equally important, the military believe they are particularly undermining of their efforts to avoid political intervention in operational decision-making.[5] Consequently, from the outset of a campaign, Media Operations work will incorporate tactic definitions to undermine critical media definitions that may arise in the future. This is predicated on the belief that the first definition will be the most enduring and against which all subsequent definitions will be assessed.

Tacit definitions are particularly evident in the use of Lines to Take (LTT) and core scripts. These devices are used to reiterate the overall strategic aims but in a manner that anticipates media enquiry about certain topics or controversies. For example, in the core script for Afghanistan, definitions are explicitly constructed in response to anticipated questions regarding the motivation for involvement, the strategies for achievement and the timelines in which this can be achieved.[6] Indeed, this latter point dominates much of the script, indicating that the scale and length of the operation is believed to be the topic liable to generate the most negative reportage. Essentially, in their revealing of information about these topics in advance, political and military actors are attempting to protect against them in advance of their occurrence.

These types of technique are particularly evident at the start of an operation, at which point the military have most to gain from their assertion of the 'first' definition of a topic area. For example, and with regards to the efficacy of military equipment, during the Iraq War tactic definitions regarding the capabilities *and* shortcomings of the tank in desert conditions were incorporated from the outset. This was particularly evident in the reportage of the build-up phase, when troops were amassing on the Kuwaiti border. As one military member stated in an interview:

> The tank provides the first echelon of the fighting force. It is obviously extremely well armored, it provides mobility and it is a massive amount of firepower and it's well protected itself and therefore leads any advancing force into battle, as did the Knights of old … however, as we advance into battle, large irrigation channels will present problems – it is susceptible to getting stuck.
>
> (Major Tim Brown, *Fighting the War*, BBC 2, June 2003)

Definitions such as these are illustrative of how, by drawing attention to the possible deficiencies of military equipment, the military attempt to preempt criticism of equipment failings prior to their occurrence. Moreover, by drawing attention to their awareness of these potential eventualities the military also attempt to invoke impressions of 'professionalism' and 'preparedness'. Similarly, from the outset of a campaign, definitions will pay heed to concerns about potential casualties, but in doing so incorporate into the definition the procedures and resources invested in minimizing this risk. Thus, during the Iraq War the military organized facilities for the media to observe and report on the processes by which they managed incidents of military casualties and death. This included the observation of troops sorting through 'in the event of death' letters and the interviewing of military personnel about their feelings regarding the possibility of death or injury during the operation (see, in particular, *Fighting the War*, BBC 2, June 2003).

With regard to the war in Afghanistan, tacit definitions have also incorporated the potential for civilian casualties. Crucially, however, these are constructed as most likely to result from insurgent actions 'deliberately undertaken in populated areas' to undermine coalition efforts.[7] By tacitly constructing the likelihood of incurring civilian casualties in this way, the military can 'fall back' on this definition as a means with which to protect their own credibility when casualties are incurred, particularly if there are no other means through which the media can verify the information provided. Essentially, 'tacit' definitions like these are employed to preempt potential critical definitions in the future, in this case by highlighting the possibility of death or injury from the outset of the operation. Further, they can also help to characterize soldiering activity as dangerous and risk-taking, while portraying the military organization as one that cares and is sensitive to the needs of its members and the civilian population in the theater of operations, both of which may assist with the bolstering of support among the internal and UK home audience.

In the use of tacit and preventative definitions, the military reveal information about potentially discreditable situations to inoculate against them in advance of their occurrence (Goffman, 1963). This voluntary disclosure is a means of managing information that has the capacity to generate unfavorable impressions if exposed at a later date. By revealing discreditable information through tacit definitions, the military therefore attempt to limit the potential damage the information may cause in the future. However, in accordance with Goffman's notion of strategic interaction, the success of the communication of these definitions – or control moves – is wholly contingent on unsuspecting or acquiescent media observers to willingly communicate these definitions to audiences. Yet, if in their assessment of military definitions media observers believe the military are attempting to misrepresent the 'reality' of the situation, or define it in a manner from which they clearly stand to profit, they may not always be willing to communicate it. As one Channel 4 correspondent stated of the arrival of the Galahad in Um Qsar during the Iraq War:

> It did happen, it's true but it was a sort of stage-managed event. I didn't even go because I knew it would be what's known in the trade delightfully as a 'Mongolian pig fuck'. There would be thousands of journalists all over, they [the military] bussed them in from Kuwait City, it was mad, but in propaganda terms probably quite sensible.
>
> (Channel 4 correspondent, interview data)

If definitions are suspected but still communicated, the media may simply undermine the definition by demonstrating their suspicion in the communicative process. For example, when the military use the term 'friendly fire' to define incidents where a member of a coalition team fires upon another member of the same team, the media often refer to it as 'so-called friendly fire' as a means by which to question the symbolism associated with the phrase 'friendly' (see, in particular, *BBC 1 News* and *Channel 4 News*, 31 March 2003). Similarly, when the media utilize military footage in reportage, they usually highlight its non-objectivity by stating, either through captions or commentary, that the imagery cannot be independently verified as accurate.

In the knowledge that they can be used as conduits for military definitions, the media assert their own independence and neutrality by either not communicating the definition or challenging it through reinterpretation. In so doing they avoid the generation of impressions that they are being manipulated by the politically persuasive practices of the military. Consequently, preventative or tacit definitions are not always successful. Indeed, despite their efforts to preempt accusations of 'mission creep' during the Iraq War by incorporating long timescales into their tacit definitions, these were rarely reported by the media. Instead, three weeks into the war, the media coverage suggested the campaign was 'dragging' and running into difficulties (*BBC News* and *Channel 4 News*, 31 March 2003).[8] Essentially, and in accordance with the media's own requirements, military definitions that warn of potential disaster are not newsworthy until disaster actually occurs (see also Moeller, 1999; Brauman, 1993).[9] The success of tacit definitions to preempt unfavorable coverage and definitional disruption is therefore unpredictable.

Competing definitions

As stated earlier, the military attempt to reveal and conceal information about their activities through linguistic, visual and narrative control moves. In an environment where technological advances allow the media to cover events as they unfold, and in accordance with the media 'flash to bang' demands for constant information, ongoing and evolving tactical activities must therefore be defined as they occur. Implicitly, and in line with the traditional reticence that is still evident in Media Operations practice, the military would undoubtedly rather conceal information about their tactical actions until definitions can be formulated with some certainty. However, owing to the nature of the environment in which they operate and the contest of assessment that occurs with media observers, the delivery of military definitions requires speed. In their own terms, the military state that they can win or lose the definition of an incident in the first hour.[10] When incidents are not defined, the military believe that the media are more likely to engage in speculation regarding what may be happening in the battle space, or regarding the military's motives for concealing information. Thus, they argue that they always attempt to provide definitions and explanations of situations as quickly as possible.

Concurrently, they argue that when working toward media demands for immediacy they are limited in their capacity to ensure the accuracy and consistency of
definitions of tactical activity due to the speed at which a battle may evolve.[11] In
these cases they argue it is not uncommon for the 'first' report of front-line activity
to be wrong, or to change within a matter of hours, given that it is based upon
rapidly changing scenarios.[12] As one Channel 4 correspondent stated of his experience of the inaccuracy of information he was given during the Iraq War:

> Day after day after day we were told Um Qsar had fallen and Um Qsar
> hadn't fallen. Then day after day we were told that Safwan had fallen. It
> hadn't. Then we were told Az Zubayr day after day had. It hadn't. We killed
> Chemical Ali and then last week, oh no we haven't. As Colonel Chris
> Vernon said 'Well we are 99.9% sure that we killed him' well it was the 1%
> wasn't it – I'm sorry, egg on face.... Then we got to Basra and it all got
> completely silly, first of all there was the rebellion that never existed. Then
> there was their firing on people leaving Basra, which they weren't. Then they
> are leaving in droves from Basra to escape, which they weren't. Then the
> tank column escaping from Basra which didn't happen, or it certainly didn't
> happen in the numbers like they said it would.
>
> (Channel 4 correspondent, interview data)

While this level of inaccurate information provision generates a potential for
competing definitions, it must also be borne in mind that there may be short-term
strategic and tactical benefits in the dissemination of inaccurate 'first reports' to
and through the media. With reference to the example above, the military certainly stood to gain from the mass communication of definitions that stated Um
Qsar had fallen and that Basra had incurred an uprising. Both of these definitions
imply military victory, or progression toward victory. Moreover, if such definitions are communicated at the 'right' time, the action may have indeed occurred
by the time the inaccuracy of the original definition is exposed. More important
– but related – is the degree to which these types of definitions may be deliberate
control moves on behalf of the military to not only assert a particular reality, but
to encourage it to happen. In other words, to assert that an uprising was taking
place in Basra may be a deliberate and calculated act on behalf of the military to
generate an uprising in Basra by engendering local support through the mass
media. As one critic stated:

> If word comes out in CENTCOM that there is an uprising against Saddam
> Hussein's regime, they can be thinking and hoping that the idea will be
> picked up on and that the local people will build on that and the information
> will become a reality, even if it never necessarily existed in the first place.
>
> (*Correspondent: War Spin*, BBC 2, 18 May 2003)

Indeed, similar communications were used in Sierra Leone in 1999. The military disseminated definitions of themselves as 'fighters' in local Sierra Leone

media to try to mobilize the local civilian population in the quashing of rebel forces.[13] In fact, at that stage their official mandate was to embark on an evacuation operation (rather than fight). But, by circulating definitions to the contrary, the military hoped they would unite the locals in their resistance to and rallying against the rebels.[14] It is therefore important to recognize that it may occasionally be in the military's interest to encourage – or certainly not discourage – the communication of 'first report' definitions, or exploit rumors that may further their own tactical interests (Shibutani, 1966).

Despite this, and not unsurprisingly, the common military response is to argue that their dissemination of inaccurate definitions is due to media demands for constant information in rapidly evolving situations.[15] Yet, in their articulation of responses like this, the military are offering further evidence of the degree to which their interactions with the media are underpinned by the contest of assessment that exists between them. Moreover, as the above quote suggests, the provision of consistently inaccurate information can incur significant risks for the military in terms of their impression management work. When offering a definition that is later exposed to be untrue, they risk undermining the integrity of not only *that* definition but *all* subsequent definitions. So, on the one hand, the military dependence on the media creates an environment in which they will attempt to court them to secure the communication of their control moves. On the other, in so doing they create a dynamic of competition and resistance among media observers who, if in their assessment of the environment suspect that the military are employing 'control moves', may engage in other, counteracting moves as a means with which to penetrate the 'staging' of the definition and uncover what is being concealed or obscured (Goffman, 1969).

Goffman terms these 'uncovering moves', by which observers attempt to expose what they consider to be the real facts of a misrepresented situation. Effectively, when the media engage in uncovering moves they are attempting to reveal what they believe is being concealed by 'stage managed' events. This can present significant challenges for the military in their attempts to define their activities on their own terms. For example, one military Media Operations member stated that if the media asked to visit the mobile grave or body bag unit during operations he would be reluctant to agree on the basis that the resulting reportage would define military actions in terms of death and destruction. However, to refuse media access may generate an impression that the military were expecting to incur large-scale casualties because they had attempted to conceal the body bag facility.[16] Under these conditions, neither revealing further, nor concealing, will assist with reinstating the original definition.

Thus, in the contest of assessment that occurs between the military and media, it is nearly always to the media's advantage to engage with 'staged events' and control moves as they may be able to acquire 'uncovering' information as a result. For instance, during the Iraq War, when attending a military media facility, a Channel 4 correspondent stated that he was able to unwittingly observe an alternative definition of the situation to the one the military were attempting to communicate:

Just after the war they took us, in the helicopter and flew us in to the Ramal-
lah oil field to look at the gas oil separation plants, which were very important things. Now what they wanted was for us to go in and find the good
news story, i.e. here they [British Troops] are, they've secured these things.
Well actually when we got there, there were one or two soldiers but the
place is far from secure, anyone could come along at any time and sabotage
it. I look around and there's a sabotage of a pipe as we speak. This was not
the story they wanted told, but it was the reality we found on the ground.
Now if you are a half way, woken up, mature journalist it's pretty easy to
tell the public 'this is the story they wanted telling, nothing wrong with that,
but in fact this is what I found on the ground this morning'. So in a weird
kind of way, these kinds of PR jaunts, it was always worth going. They were
always quite valid because OK, it was clearly the menu of the day this is
what we are gonna set up for you but this is Iraq, you never know how it's
really gonna work out on the ground.

(Channel 4 correspondent, interview data)

In this way, the military can unintentionally and unknowingly reveal information
about their activities through their use of control moves and staged events.

Perhaps the clearest way in which media observers utilize uncovering moves
is through the exposure of inconsistencies in the military 'team performance'.
Due to the increasing multilateral nature of war operations, effective 'stage management' of definitions is contingent on the dramaturgical cooperation of all military and political members if a given definition of a situation is to be convincing
(see Goffman, 1959: 88). Essentially, a united 'front' is critical, not least because
the military are particularly conscious that the media will look for fractures in
the team performance for their own purposes: 'Recent campaigns have highlighted the need to harmonize key media messages and themes to counter the
media's tendency to expose differences and to exploit these for news purposes'
(JWP 3-45, 2001: 1-3).

Yet, in light of the number of parties involved and their potentially divergent
objectives, disagreements or conflict between 'team members' can easily arise.[17]
These must be suppressed or concealed in the team performance if the definition
is to succeed. Despite the military's efforts to do so, however, and by virtue of
their engagement in strategic interaction with media observers, there are times
when the media utilize counteracting moves as a means with which to penetrate
this 'staging' and uncover fractures that would otherwise be obscured (Goffman,
1969). For example, after a friendly fire incident in the Iraq War, both Channel 4
and the BBC reported that British troops expressed increasing anger toward the
US military. This was supported by an interview with an injured British soldier,
who allegedly accused the US pilots of being 'cowboys', 'trigger happy' and
'having no regard for human life' (*BBC 1 News* and *Channel 4 News*, 31 March
2003). Around the same time, a British military spokesman was also reported
criticizing the US military news management team for lacking in efficiency
(*Correspondent: War Spin*, BBC 2, 18 May 2003). Moreover, the BBC claimed

that a British political advisor had complained that the US news team was not 'up to the job' and that 'the Jessica Lynch presentation was embarrassing'[18] (*Correspondent: War Spin*, BBC 2, 18 May 2003). Such inconsistencies in the united front are indicative of the potential discord between the coalition partners.

Certainly, with regards to Afghanistan, the military argue that a lack of cohesion between NATO forces, and the absence of a definitive, integrated approach to Media Operations among contributing nations has generated inconsistencies in 'unified' definitions.[19] They also concede that, at times, their political Afghan partners have undermined their capacity to generate a cohesive 'front' for the NATO operation.[20] In these circumstances, the military are particularly vulnerable to media uncovering moves that render visible the fractured team performance. For example, when NATO forces killed a number of Afghan civilians in 2009 during an airstrike in Kunduz, President Karzai was reported to have criticized NATO for needlessly causing the death of Afghan civilians through an error of judgment. When fractures like this are exposed in the media, (re)defining techniques typically stress the anomaly of the individual (or the action), as 'rogue'.[21] Certainly, President Karzai has been represented as having 'rogue' characteristics – evident in accusations of corruption and ineffectual governance. So, too, have a number of 'allied' members of the Afghan National Army (ANA), who the media have reported as engaging in drug taking, lacking discipline and being 'clueless' (see *BBC 1 News*, 13 August 2010).

In more extreme cases, when members of the ANA have actually attacked NATO troops, the media have variously suggested that these attacks could be due to Taliban infiltration of the ANA, behavioral problems among ANA soldiers and the mistreatment of the ANA by their NATO 'mentors' (see, in particular, *Channel 4 News*, 13 July 2010; *Guardian*, 15 July 2010). In contrast, the political military response has been to define them as the actions of a 'rogue element': 'We believe these were the actions of a lone individual who has betrayed his ISAF and Afghan comrades' (interview with military spokesman for Task Force Helmand, *Channel 4 News*, 13 July 2010). Of course, this latter example is extreme in terms of its exposure of fractures. Nonetheless, as with the others, it exemplifies the challenges the military face in concealing fractures in the team performance, while also demonstrating how, through redefining techniques, they attempt to counter media uncovering moves that expose them.

At the same time, it is noteworthy that there may be occasions when the team performance is deliberately undermined, and fractures revealed to the media intentionally. Effectively, the party involved utilizes the media to publicly assert a definition of a situation that is aligned to their own aims rather than those of the 'team'. Indeed, the examples above can be interpreted in this manner, employed by the British military to distance themselves from incidents which they believe may work to their detriment (e.g. Jessica Lynch and friendly fire incidents).

Discordance in military definitions and fractures in the team performance can, therefore, be control moves, intentionally produced to influence responses in the military's favor. For example, when two British soldiers were killed during an ambush in the Iraq war, Prime Minister Tony Blair was quick to define the incident as an 'execution' and one of a number of atrocities committed by the Iraqi Regime (*BBC News*, 27 March 2003). In contrast, the British military stated that it was difficult to prove with any certainty that an execution had taken place,[22] and publicly announced that the soldiers 'may' have been executed (*Channel 4 News*, 27 March 2003). For the military, it was important that this (re)definition was asserted in order to reassure the internal military audience, who were distressed about the fate of the soldiers and the potential risks to other military personnel in the battle space.[23] The military's desire to communicate a message of reassurance to protect morale among their own audience was therefore of greater importance than acquiescing to their political governors in the 'united front'.

Similarly, in September 2006, and in the context of increasing disillusionment with the strategic organization of the Iraq War campaign, Chief of Staff Sir General Richard Dannatt exposed a significant fracture in the political–military 'front' by campaigning in the media for better conditions for service personnel (*Daily Mail*, 12 October 2006). He justified these actions in 2009, stating they were considered and calculated and undertaken to demonstrate to military troops that he, as their general, was 'fighting their cause' (*BBC Today Programme*, 21 July 2009). Examples such as these are suggestive of how communications to one audience group may take precedence over the collaborative team performance.

In compromising the united front, and cognizant that exposure of difference is newsworthy, the military thus attempt to define, or redefine their activities in a manner that will potentially lead to the attainment of *their own* institutional goals. It is important to recognize, however, that these types of incidents are rare. Instead, fractures in the team performance and definitional inconsistencies are generally made visible by the contradictions between the need to maintain a united front and the actual realities of military work. They highlight the degree to which there are evident limitations to the military's capacity to consistently define their activities in their own terms.

In situations where contradictions and inconsistencies are exposed, the military situation can be transformed from one in which they are potentially *discreditable*, to one in which they are actually *discredited* (Goffman, 1963: 116). What results, by virtue of the contest of assessment between the military and the media, is a descent into a sequence of moves, counter-moves and adaptations as each party tries to define and redefine a situation in accordance with their own respective institutional needs. In some cases, the military may attempt to conceal additional discrediting information in what Goffman terms a 'covering move', although this usually aggravates the situation if suspected or exposed (Goffman, 1969, 1963). Similarly, military counter-moves may also involve denial, but this is only effective when there are doubts regarding the original discreditable definition (Shibutani, 1966: 200). A good illustration of this was the political and military defining of the coalition airstrike on a Baghdad market in 2003, which killed 14 Iraqi civilians. In a classic counter-move, US and UK forces initially denied involvement and instead defined it as an 'Iraqi own goal':[24] 'It is increasingly probable that this was the result of Iraqi – not coalition – action' (UK Foreign Secretary Jack Straw interviewed on *BBC 1 News*, 2 April 2003). In contrast, through an uncovering move, journalists claimed that US missile parts existed among the debris and redefined the bombing as a coalition attack on a civilian neighborhood (see *Correspondent: War Spin*, BBC 2, 18 May 2003). As one correspondent reporting in the region stated:

> The Coalition doesn't want to admit a disproportionate response – hunting Scuds in a residential neighborhood would endanger far more lives than the number endangered if Iraq actually managed to fire the missile, so settles with perpetuating a lie that the Iraqis are heartless enough to be targeting their own people for propaganda purposes.
>
> (Diary of Channel 4 correspondent during Iraq War)

Consequently, coalition forces were not only accused of the attack, but of also attempting to shift responsibility for the civilians' deaths on to the Iraqi regime. The potentially *discreditable* coalition became *discredited*. Under these conditions, it is not unusual for further defensive practices to be employed which, in conflict situations, typically involve apportioning greater blame to the adversary, or charging the adversary with having an impressive propaganda machine from which the discreditable definitions are generated and against which the public must be vigilant (see also Shibutani, 1996). Thus, in a further move that attempted to reinstate the credibility of the originally definition – for this becomes the only option available in the contest of assessment that ensues – British Secretary of Defence Geoff Hoon tried to further shift the focus of discredit to the Iraqi regime claiming that Iraqi officials had 'cleared up' the site 'to disguise their own responsibility for what took place' (*BBC 1 News*, 3 April 2003). In so doing, Hoon questioned the credibility of Iraqi accounts, and implicitly asserted that the only accurate, trustworthy and reliable facts are those that emanate from the political or military sphere: 'All of us should look very skeptically at these kinds of reports; relying only on known agreed facts' (British Secretary of Defence Geoff Hoon, *Correspondent: War Spin*, BBC 2, 18 May 2003). In this sense, 'agreed facts' becomes a pseudonym for what is actually a politically persuasive definition of a situation from which the military and politicians stand to gain.

Moreover, and indeed it is here that the contest of definitions in the strategic interaction with the media becomes more evident, discredit is also very often shifted to the media as a means with which to question the validity or authority of their reportage. Certainly, Hoon attempted this by calling into question 'these kind of reports' and suggesting media 'facts' were speculative (*BBC 1 News*, 3 April 2003). In the same manner, UK Forces Minister Adam Ingram suggested that media interviews with Trooper Finney, the survivor of the friendly fire incident, were neither objective nor appropriate in light of Finney's recent traumatic experience (*BBC 1 News* and *Channel 4 News*, 31 March 2003). Likewise, Al Jazeera was heavily criticized for their reportage of the killing of two British soldiers. The content of the report, which showed Iraqi civilians celebrating and beating the bodies of the soldiers, was particularly discrediting for the military. It undermined their definitions of being a proactive and protective force, not least because it was clear from the report that they were unaware of the men's deaths until the broadcast (see, in particular, *ITV News*, 25 March 2003). In response, the military stated that Al Jazeera was especially unbalanced (*Channel 4 News*, 27 March 2003). All of these examples, but especially this last one, highlight the degree to which in their attempts to discredit the media (or indeed other parties), political and military definers incorporate a tacit stigmatism of relevant parties in the discrediting definitions. In so doing, discrediting definitions have the dual purpose of not only shifting the discredit, but also compensating for the potential of similar occurrences in the future.

It is through these defensive practices that the military attempt to manage the discredit generated by competing definitions or the exposure, disclosure or uncovering of information that is detrimental to their impression management performances. Primarily, they are reactive and used when other more proactive defining strategies have failed. Most importantly, however, they illustrate how the military are limited in their capacity to achieve their impression management aims as a result of their strategic interaction with media observers. Ultimately, the success of the military's defining strategies is founded on the degree to which they are able to control and manage the information made available to media observers. It is in this attempt to control, and by virtue of their being few alternate sources of information, that the media engage in counteracting moves to penetrate any potential 'staging' of a military definition. When successful, the military situation can be quickly transformed to a discredited one, which in turn produces further moves and counter-moves through which the reinstatement of credibility is attempted. Importantly, all of the actions and strategic interactions apparent in the formation and management of definitions are made relative to a world that has already been generated by the interaction between the military and the media. In other words, without a military or media presence in the environment, or the contest of assessment that arises in this interaction, the interplay of moves and the potential for competing definitions would not exist. It is in this way that the military's endeavors to reveal, conceal and redefine information about activities proactively contributes to the social construction of the environment in which they operate. Similarly, in the symbiosis that exists between the military and the media and the resulting counter-moves and adaptations, the media also contribute to the social construction of this environment, particularly in their attempt to 'uncover' information in accordance with their own institutional needs. What results is the obscuring of the reality of a situation as it becomes increasingly lost in a descent into competing definitions and contestation between both parties.

8 Performing war
Bounded impression management

In the previous chapter, strategic interaction was used to explain how the military define their activities for impression management purposes. The focus of this chapter is the performance of Media Operations impression management. In this sense, this chapter continues to employ the artificial distinction between 'defining situations' in, and the 'performance' of, Media Operations work despite their interdependence. In pursuing the distinction here, this chapter is focused upon *how* the military attempt to secure the communication of their definitions through particular performative aspects of impression management. Drawing on Meyrowitz's (1985) concept of the information system, the first part of the chapter discusses how we can understand the performance of military impression management in accordance with the military's ability to control patterns of access to information about their activities. In particular, the information system allows us to consider the degree to which military impression management performances are no longer confined to direct, co-present interaction with media observers. A distinction is thus made between impression management that is performed in direct, co-present interaction with media observers, and impression management performed in non-co-present interaction with media observers. It is the former of these – bounded impression management – that forms the basis of this chapter, where co-present interaction affords the military distinct performance and strategic interaction opportunities.

The information system

As is now evident, the military classify their Media Operations audiences as members of the public, rather than members of the media. Media Operations work is therefore predicated on a mediated relationship with their audience, enacted through the media. Because Goffman's (1959) dramaturgical analysis is tied to physical locations, a literal application of impression management to Media Operations limits our understanding of social interaction enacted with and through the media. In contrast, Meyrowitz's (1985) concept of the 'information system' is a more inclusive concept through which we can understand how people acquire information about the military both in and beyond co-present interactions. The information system comprises patterns of access to social information about the actions of others, that is: 'All that people are capable of knowing about the behavior and actions of themselves and others ... access to each other's social performances' (Meyrowitz, 1985: 37). In this way, as a conceptual tool, the information system allows us to consider the effect on military impression management of the increased patterns of access to information about military activities as a result of multiple, global competitive media outlets and diverse information sources. Moreover, the concept of the information system also better elucidates the importance of strategic interaction to Media Operations impression management for it is through strategic interaction that the military attempt to reveal and conceal certain aspects of their behavior.

Essentially, strategic interaction is founded on the interplay of three principles: the 'covered', the 'cover' and 'uncovering perception' (Goffman, 1969: 23). The covered represents what a subject – in this case the military – is concealing. The cover is the means through which they are able to hide the concealed. Uncovering perception is the means through which media observers are able to 'uncover' the covered, which here is represented by the patterns of access to information about the military available to the media in the information system. For Goffman, both the covered and the cover are affected by uncovering perception. In short, the multiple means through which the media can acquire information about military activities has a direct influence on the military's ability to conceal particular types of information through impression management performances and strategic interaction. It is with this in mind that the organization of Media Operations performances is interrogated and explained in the remainder of this chapter. The concept of the information system therefore functions as a means through which we can understand *both* co-present and non-co-present impression management. It is also a tool with which to assess how the media's ability to gain information about military activities beyond co-present impression management affects the military's attempts to reveal and conceal information through strategic interaction.

Bounded impression management

'Bounded impression management' is an analytical concept developed to describe the co-present performance of Media Operations impression management. It is termed 'bounded' here because it is place-bound and performed in direct interaction with media observers. Bounded impression management comprises the bulk of Media Operations work. It therefore encompasses all those facilities that the military organize in the theater of operations, namely: press information centers, media facilities, escorting and embedding. While each facility offers different performative and strategic interaction opportunities, they are all oriented toward revealing and concealing specific information about operational activity. Bounded impression management performances consist of a 'front' and 'back' region in which the performance is enacted and constructed, respectively. In this sense, Goffman's (1959) understanding of impression management describes this aspect of the information system in an unproblematic way.

In accordance with Goffman's dramaturgical perspective, the front region is where the military act out their team performance with the use of expressive equipment, such as appearance, setting and manner, to define the situation for those journalists who observe it (Goffman, 1959). Goffman defines the front region (or front stage) as: 'That part of an individual's performance that regularly functions in a general and fixed fashion to define the situation for those who observe the performance' (Goffman, 1959: 32). For Goffman, it is usually – although not always – place-bound, whereupon leaving the 'setting' the performance is terminated. For the military, these place-bound settings typically include press conferences, press briefings, interviews and media facilities. All of these performances are structured to provide registered journalists with ongoing information about strategic and tactical activity throughout the duration of the operation. Press conference and briefings in particular are organized in response to incidents that need defining, or operational developments that the military consider worthy of defining for impression management purposes.

In an attempt to secure the effective communication of definitions, bounded impression management performances are organized around meeting the information-gathering needs of the media, but in a manner that suits military requirements. Press conferences and briefings are scheduled to occur at regular intervals, usually each morning, lunchtime and evening, and especially in accordance with the needs of television news broadcasts.[1] Indeed, press information centers are deliberately constructed to encourage media attendance and are therefore built to provide comfortable and well-located facilities for media observers in the hope that they will utilize the information provided. Similarly, media facility performances are constructed so as to meet the media demand for visual imagery. While performances across all these Media Operations facilities may vary in their format and setting, the military attempt to coordinate all their performances in order that, collectively, they fit together as a whole. In so doing, they endeavor to generate an emergent impression that appears to reflect a reality in its own right (see Goffman, 1959: 85). For this reason, the military stress that the credibility of definitions resides in team performances in which military members collaborate to project and sustain definitions. This is evident in the discourses surrounding Media Operations work, such as: 'We all need to be saying the same thing' and 'A number of people saying the same thing is better that one person saying it a number of times.' It is through these team performances in the front region that the military attempt to generate the impression of a cohesive 'front'.

In contrast, the back region is where military definitions are constructed and fabricated, and to which media observers have restricted access. Goffman defines the back region as:

> a place, relative to a given performance where the impression fostered by the performance is knowingly contradicted as a matter of course … it is here that the capacity of a performance to express something beyond itself may

be painstakingly fabricated; it is here that illusions and impressions are openly constructed.

(Goffman, 1959: 114)

It is in this back region that facts regarding the construction of the performance and 'front' are suppressed. For the military, back region activity typically consists of planning and preparing Media Operations work in advance of the front region performance. In particular, military members are trained to identify the 'issues' and 'threads' that have emerged or are emerging in current media coverage of the operation. This is done through ongoing monitoring and analysis of newspapers and television broadcasts in the back region and in the MoD.[2] Front region performances are then organized in accordance with these identified factors, and definitions constructed around key themes and messages that the military wish to communicate. In addition, back region activity is concerned with the coordination and harmonization of information from which collaborative team performances can be enacted. As such, team members will collectively engage in pre-conference meetings, advisory sessions between MoD and theater-based Media Operations personnel, or regular 'early bird round tables', where the military debate and organize the media issues to be tackled that day.[3]

To this end, performances are often constructed a day in advance,[4] around pre-defined topics that have been identified as relevant and important to overall impression management aims. As one journalist stated of his experience in the British field press information center during the Iraq War:

> They used to have this white board under the camo netting in the desert and they actually wrote 'menu' on the top and there was 'today's story will be'. We will lay on a trip for you to see whatever the good news story of the day was.
>
> (Channel 4 correspondent, interview data)

It is through these 'menus' that the military attempt to define and control the definitions communicated by the media. In addition, back region work is focused on preempting unfavorable definitions in advance of their occurrence. In particular, it is in the back region that the military anticipate potential contingencies and definitional disruptions. From this they construct tacit definitions to be incorporated into front region military performances. This latter point is illustrative of the degree to which back region work is not only concerned with the advance planning of a particular performance on a daily basis, but with the planning of performances and definitions over the length of an entire operation so that performances are consistent and coherent throughout.

Regulation of contact

In the distinction between the front and back regions, and because media observers have restricted access to the back region, the military have the ability to limit their interaction with media observers to front region performances. Consequently, they can restrict the possibility of contaminating a performance by maintaining control over the patterns of access to the more 'covered' aspects of their Media Operations work. As Goffman states: 'If perception is a form of contact, then control of what is perceived is control over contact that is made, and the limitation and regulation of what is shown is a limitation and regulation of contact' (Goffman, 1959: 74).

This regulation of contact is a key characteristic of military bounded impression management and is important to the effective impression management performance. By keeping their back regions private, the military are able to script performances in advance and consider how best to stage them. Moreover, because of the temporal structure of press conferences, briefings and media facilities military performers are rarely in the continuous presence of media observers. Instead, they have the ability to limit their co-present interaction with media observers to set times and set formats, thereby reducing opportunities for the corruption of a previously prepared performance.

Regulation of contact is further achievable in the confines of each facility. For example, press information centers will have their own specific remit, and while the military attempt to coordinate information across all centers, information will only be provided for those contained or registered within a particular center. As such, according to one military member, the field press information center near Basra during the Iraq War did not function as a general information provider for all media observers. Instead, it was specifically designed to accommodate and facilitate performances for the 40 journalists that were located within it. In this way the military were able to retain control over access to definitions through the regulation of correspondents and the types of information they were able to obtain.

One of the significant ways the military are able to initiate and maintain regulation of contact with media observers is through the registration and accreditation of correspondents prior to their arrival in a theater of operations. All correspondents have to be registered with the military in order to seek admission to any of the Media Operations press centers, facilities and embed opportunities. Registration and accreditation are only available under the provisions of the MoD's *Green Book*, which outlines the working arrangements under which the military engage with the media during operations.[5] The *Green Book* is essentially a statement of intent on behalf of the military, but also serves as a formal articulation of the restrictions the media will be required to operate under. Such restrictions allow the military to limit and control the number of media observers attending their front region performances and the capacity in which they attend:

Accreditation will be at the discretion of the MoD, which reserves the right to decide on the numbers and to withhold or withdraw accreditation ... the MoD will decide on the number of correspondents that can be safely and appropriately supported on any particular operation or facility.... Where possible, representatives of the UK national and regional press, news agencies, broadcasters, specialist media and international media, will be included in each operation or facility with the aim of ensuring fair and balanced representation from each category of media.

(Green Book, 2010: 8)

Although decisions about the selection of particular correspondents are left to the relevant media organizations and editors, this initial accreditation process (and the threat of its withdrawal) allows the military ultimate control over media access to their front region performances. This has a number of additional subsidiary advantages for the military.

First, by virtue of the limited numbers of media observers, the 'pooling' of information is required. Pooling occurs when the demand for information exceeds the supply of information for individual journalists. In these circumstances, material produced by media observers within a Media Operations facility is shared and made available to all media outlets on request (*Green Book*, 2010: 14). In this regard, the pooling of information is considered to help pacify competition among media observers, thereby reducing the potential for speculation and rumor.[6] Moreover, pooling tends to unify a military definition across a number of media outlets, generating an impression of consistency in the military performance.

Second, as a condition of accreditation, media observers have to adhere to military embargoes and censorship if they are to remain in the hosting facility and gain access to information. This requires the submission of all media material for military security checking. The military argue that this is justifiable on the basis that media observers may unwittingly make public information that is of benefit to the enemy, compromise the lives of military members (or civilians) or endanger an operation (*Green Book*, 2010: 15). In particular, the *Green Book* cites a number of specific operational subjects that media observers must not include in reportage because they will compromise security, including: the composition of a force, details of military movements, military plans or intentions, tactics, details of defensive positions, methods of camouflage, weapon capabilities, force protection measures, names of individual service personnel, prisoners of war and casualties (*Green Book*, 2010: 14). It is noteworthy that some of these subject areas correspond directly with those the military anticipate will generate unfavorable coverage, and around which they construct tacit definitions, such as equipment and casualties. To disallow media reportage of these topics, or to tailor coverage through vetting procedures, allows the military to (re)define a situation in their own terms.

In light of this, some media observers suggest that vetting restrictions are used to prevent the communication of particular types of media coverage. For example, one media observer argued that in Iraq, coverage that ran contrary to the military's aims incurred the threat of de-registration:

We were not allowed to take any pictures, or describe British soldiers carrying guns.... I was told that there was a decision, made by Downing Street, that the British military were to go to any lengths not to portray British fighting men and women as fighters, they wanted to have them there as 'nation builders', that they weren't going to be killing people. The media minders would get very upset with you and threats were leveled against you that you would be dis-embedded.

(Tom Copetas, *Correspondent: War Spin*, BBC 2, 18 May 2003)

Of course, to allow the communication of media reportage that portrays soldiers as fighters does – to some extent – undermine the military ability to evoke impressions of their work within the 'liberation' framework. At the same time, in accordance with the *Green Book*, the filming of military equipment undermines operational security because it makes available to the enemy information that they could use to their advantage. Thus, although the military claim that reporting restrictions are justifiable on the grounds of operational security, because of the contest of assessment between the media and the military, it becomes increasingly difficult to ascertain if, and when, operational security may be being used as a cover for impression management purposes. If, as some suggest, the military are risk averse in their dealings with the media, the vetting of reportage (justified through operational security) becomes a key device to avoid the potential threats that media coverage may generate (Bracken, 2009). Reliant on their military hosts for information, media observers have little choice but to acquiesce to vetting requests if they believe that they will be denied access to information in the future.

Indeed, in their strategic interaction with the media, the military are cognizant that there are few alternate sources for the kind of information they are able to provide. They therefore see the media as reliant upon them in a manner that permits them to manage, with relative ease, the types of information the media acquire and communicate.[7] This belief is particularly evident in statements like 'They need us as much as we need them',[8] but is also apparent in the accounts of Media Operations staff. As one military member suggested, media facilities are organized on the basis of what the military want to show the media, rather than what the media want to see.[9] In this respect, by virtue of being the information provider, the military are able to deny media observers access to those aspects of their activities they wish to keep concealed. As one correspondent stated:

The freedom of movement was completely restricted, that is clearly a form of censorship, it is clearly a form of preventing you getting information independently ... our movements were censored. Our ability to work independently was non-existent, we were totally and wholly dependent on information that we were spoon fed by the military, we didn't have any other access to information. You couldn't walk outside the camp on your own because it was deemed unsafe, against the rules and all the rest of it ... so you don't have to censor with a blue pen. You censor by saying 'There is no vehicle available, sorry ... there is still no vehicle available, we hope to have a vehicle tomorrow morning' that's far more effective than blue pen censorship which is largely a myth, it doesn't happen any more.

(Channel 4 correspondent, interview data)

The military account for these kinds of restrictions of movement on the grounds that they are responsible for the protection of registered journalists. At the same time, it presents them with opportunities to prevent media observation of their back region activities. In this sense, the regulation of contact in bounded impression management performances has the dual purpose of protecting the 'covered' back region *and* increasing the potential for military definitions, performed through the front region 'cover' to be consistently unified in a number of media outlets.

While the military are able to restrict their contact with media observers through bounded impression management, there will still be times when they are in the presence of media observers beyond set times and performance formats. In these situations, their interactions must be consistent with the rehearsed 'front' if the generation of competing definitions and exposure of back region activity is to be avoided. This 'front' can be difficult to maintain in hosting situations where the military might be required to share informal settings with media observers, and where informal chat can undermine the credibility of the front region performances. As ITN's Romilly Weeks stated of her experience:

> If you just chatted to the soldiers informally they would always say very interesting things like 'yes, we are scared', 'no, we haven't done this before', 'I don't want to die in Iraq' or whatever. But, what he [military media advisor] would do is pick out five people that he wanted me to talk to, line them all up, and brief them beforehand.... It became, everyday, the same line: 'We are here to do a job.'
>
> (Romilly Weeks, *The War We Never Saw: The True Face of War*,
> Channel 4, 5 June 2003)

The military's inability to strictly regulate contact across *all* settings can therefore compromise the integrity of performances. This is particularly the case with embedding where, in contrast to the strict differentiation between front and back regions in other facilities, the front and back regions of embedding are less clearly defined. Indeed, embeds are required to use basic military facilities alongside military members when accompanying them to front-line activities, consequently compromising the opportunities for the military to engage in back region work. Given that there is less scope for regulated contact, there is also a greater risk of the media being privy to actions that the military would prefer not to have communicated. With a less clearly defined back region, the military are unable to 'stage manage' tactical activities or their own 'team' behavior in the same way as permitted by bounded performances in press information centers and media facilities. In recognition of this, the military endeavor to limit the amount of time a media observer embeds with a particular unit, not least because growing familiarity with media observers may encourage military members to 'drop their guard' and thereby expose the back region.[10] Moreover, these liabilities are further offset by the military's ability to control and vet communicated reports, and to allocate embeds to military units with specific, perhaps less dangerous, operational remits. To this end, opportunities to embed are only likely to be provided in operations where the calculated risk of defeat is extremely minimal.

The balancing of these risks provides the military with distinct impression management opportunities through embedding, primarily because the performance is not considered to be militarily generated, but to arise from the media observer's experience. In this sense, embedding is a naïve move in strategic interaction with media observers, which Goffman (1969: 11) defines as 'the assessment the observer makes of the subject when the observer believes that the subject can be taken as he appears'. In the naïve move, all suspicion of stage management is eradicated because the environment appears to be naturally occurring. As such, embed reportage invokes impressions of authenticity. Moreover, soldiers are not required to explicitly engage in impression management performances because journalists are essentially doing this work for them. In the literal and metaphorical shadowing of the military, the story is told from the soldier's perspective. In essence, the true performer is the media observer. This is considered to be distinctly advantageous for the military because, in their own words, 'You let them get on with it.'[11] Favorable impressions of military activity can thus be generated and sustained through the journalist's participation, as his or her experience serves as a 'front' for the military. This is further reinforced by the fact that embeds are not, without prior agreement, permitted to 'cover events from the opposing side at any stage' (*Green Book*, 2010: 13). Consequently, definitions of tactical activities, although emanating from the media, are predominantly from the military's perspective.

Each of these bounded impression management facilities offers distinct defining and performing opportunities for the military. In their appreciation of the kind of information the media require, the military essentially set the stage in advance through bounded impression management performances. In so doing, they are able to exert some control over the definitions communicated through the media. In this sense, all bounded impression management performances are 'control moves' in the strategic interaction that exists between military performers and media observers. As control moves, bounded performances are consciously and intentionally produced to evoke impressions from which the military stand to gain, particularly the generation of belief and action, and the realization of military goals. In addition, the effective performance of these 'control moves' is founded upon the ability of the military to subdue challenges to definitions. Hence, in an effort to maintain the integrity and authority of the performance, bounded impression management control moves also incorporate a number of other strategic interaction moves with the media. Through these moves, the military attempt to generate impressions among media observers of cooperation and credibility while also exerting some control over the definitions communicated.

Strategic interaction: honesty and secrecy

Owing to their ability to keep their back region work private, the patterns of access to information about military activity available to media observers are limited to front region performances, which act as a 'cover'. By virtue of the military being the primary – and sometimes only – information source, media observers tend to be dependent on them for information in bounded impression management facilities. It is under these conditions that strategic interaction is enacted and the contest of assessment generated. Appreciating that this contest of assessment will occur, the military incorporate a number of other strategic moves into their performance as a means with which to try to keep some information concealed while revealing other information through front region performances. In particular, the following discussion considers how the military employ honesty, open secrecy and the sharing of secrets as particular interaction moves through which they can protect their definitions.

The significance that the military attach to honest and open engagement with media observers has arisen from their appreciation that obstructive, dishonest and secretive interaction only contributes to the view of the military as controlling, uncooperative and potentially manipulative (JDP 3-45.1, 2007; see also Dandeker, 2000; Taylor, 1996; Badsey, 1994, 1996, 2001). In this way, and in acknowledgment of previous tensions with the media, they try to perceive their Media Operations work from the point of view of media observers in order to have some control over it. Honest and open engagement can therefore be seen as a form of strategic interaction through which the military attempt to generate the impression of trust among media observers. Honesty acts as a counter-uncovering move through which the military attempt to allay media suspicion of their definitions. Honesty is thus used in an attempt to preempt media 'uncovering moves' that are generally enacted by a suspicious media. To this end, military performers explicitly reveal information about the aims of back region work in bounded performances. This is described in the following account from a journalist located in a military press information center during the Iraq War:

> He [military spokesman] is a smart, bright guy and very good at his job, but very open about his job. He didn't sit around and bullshit you, he said 'I'm here to get positive coverage. I am not gonna lie to you, I'm not gonna say things which are untrue unless I genuinely believe them to be true.' So, he was completely open about it. In times gone by perhaps people would have been less open about it and actually less good at their job, you know ... he'd say 'No we are not gonna take you to things which are bad news, we are gonna take you to see things which are good news.'
>
> (Channel 4 correspondent, interview data)

By openly admitting that Media Operations work is centrally concerned with obtaining positive coverage of their activities, the military performer utilizes honesty as a control move through which trust can be elicited. For the military, practicing this kind of openness in performances is considered pivotal to sustaining credible relations with the media.[12] By generating an impression of honesty and trust through strategic interactions, the military attempt to transcend the suspicion with which the media act toward their definitions, or have acted toward their definitions in the past. It is within this overall framework of honesty and openness that two further moves, in the form of open secrecy and sharing secrets are enacted in ongoing interaction with media observers.

Open secrecy is where a subject – in this case the military performer – makes no effort to prevent the observer from perceiving that they are being kept in the dark (see Goffman, 1969: 14). In bounded impression management performances, open secrecy can be seen to be both a covering and counter-uncovering move in the sense that it is used to conceal information *and* alleviate media suspicion simultaneously. While the military do not use the term 'open secrecy', these principles are articulated in their emphasis on honesty and openness. In practical terms, open secrecy requires Media Operations staff to be open about concealing information from the media; a gesture they would previously have avoided. They therefore incorporate into performances explanations regarding why certain information needs to remain 'secret'. Through open secrecy the military attempt to differentiate for media observers 'secret' information and information that may previously have been kept secret for impression management purposes. Secret information is typically described by the military as necessarily secret to protect operational security. Operational security therefore *can* act as a 'cover' for information the military wish to keep concealed. However, it is a cover that the military recognize may be suspected by media observers if it is employed too often or inappropriately. As such, the military are instructed not to use operational security as an unnecessary 'cover' with which to hide information that does not need to be concealed, or which can be explained in other ways. In this way, the military attempt to protect the integrity of operational security as a cover when it is, or needs to be, employed, to further allay media suspicion of its use.

Despite this, some suggest that in their risk aversion with the media some military members will liberally use operational security as a cover to protect themselves and the operation against the potential for unfavorable coverage (see Bracken, 2009). Notwithstanding the implications of this for the strategic interaction with media observers, evidence suggests that when media observers are convinced of the tactical importance of the hidden information, the use of open secrecy can be a particularly successful means through which the military are able to conceal information.[13] As one correspondent stated: 'I didn't fanny around asking stupid questions like, "How many soldiers have you got in such and such a place?", which they are never gonna tell you 'cos it's Operational Security' (Channel 4 correspondent, interview data).

As both a covering and counter-uncovering move, open secrecy is thus integral to bounded impression management. In their strategic interaction with media observers it is a military move that attempts to encourage trust in performances while simultaneously protecting concealed information from exposure through media 'uncovering moves'.

In contrast to open secrecy – where military performers openly admit that they are concealing information – there are circumstances in which the military will share 'secret' information with media observers. Termed 'embargoes', this information is explicitly defined as information intended to aid media understanding but not intended for reportage, typically because it may jeopardize operational security. Once again, the sharing of secrets can be considered to be both a covering and counter-uncovering move. This is because the disclosure of secrets can act as a 'cover' for other concealed information, and because by sharing secret information with the media the military are effectively co-opting them in the 'cover' in an attempt to avert their suspicion. As Goffman (1963: 117) suggests, one of the ways in which one can manage the disclosure of potentially discrediting information is to draw close and co-opt those who may constitute the greatest danger. For Media Operations work and military impression management, it is the media who constitute this danger, for they control the means of communication for both military and competing definitions. Hence, the co-opting of the media through shared secrets is a means through which the military can attempt to manage this risk. In this manner, they can subtly encourage the media to become implicitly involved in the collective activity of defining military activities. To some degree, this co-opting process is formalized in the accreditation process and the registering of correspondents. In effect, although this is not necessarily its only function, the registration process forms the agreed terms on which the military attempt to co-opt the media in secret sharing. The military then have recourse should a media observer break the accreditation agreement. As the *Green Book* (2010: 16) states: 'Breaches [of embargos] will, therefore, be viewed very seriously and may result in the loss of accreditation and withdrawal of all facilities.'

In addition to co-opting the media, the sharing of secrets also provides opportunities for the military to enhance media understanding of operational activities. This is especially important for the military given that they argue there is a lack of specialist knowledge among journalists who report on their activities (JDP 3-45.1, 2007). To this end, the sharing of secrets can encourage trust in military definitions by placing them within the context of a strategic understanding of military plans and objectives. As one correspondent stated of his experience during the Iraq War:

> Did they say, 'I'll tell you this but you can't report this because it's just for your own background?' Yes. Relentlessly. Because they wanted us to have as full a strategic picture as they could give us.... I've never covered any war, ever, with the kind of real strategic understanding of what was going on all around me as I have on this one [the Iraq War] and that's where you really did get good overview and strategic view of what different troops were doing and where they were and what they were trying to achieve. And that was great. I've never had that before.
>
> (Channel 4 correspondent, interview data)

It is through this sharing of operational plans and developments that the military attempt to protect definitions from media speculation. By providing media observers with contextual information about an operation, they attempt to generate a greater, overall understanding of maneuvers and their strategic implications, something they consider vital to the avoidance of misrepresented definitions and rumor development.[14] Similarly, through this contextual information the military are able to reinforce prior and future definitions. Background information that may appear to be irrelevant or superfluous to the types of information media observers wish to obtain may therefore become integral to long-term definition construction for the military.

'Sharing secrets' is particularly important in embedding, primarily because embedding is oriented toward involving media observers in military activities so that the messages communicated cohere with the military perspective. In this respect, sharing secrets is integral to encouraging involvement and identification as a form of co-opting media observers in embedding roles. Much has been written about media observers psychologically identifying with military activities and troops when reporting from war zones (Tumber and Palmer, 2004; Morrison and Tumber, 1988; Morrison, 1994). In particular, it is suggested that adjusting to living within military units can induce a sense of participation rather than mere observation for journalists. Certainly, there is evidence to suggest that the military actively encourage identification, although they claim this is primarily to protect the security of the unit:

> FLMPs [front-line media pools] have been shown to be more effective and less of an operational risk once correspondents have become familiar in working with their assigned units in operational conditions and a degree of mutual trust has been established.
>
> (*Green Book*, 2003: 43)

At the same time, media identification is clearly beneficial to military impression management work. By involving media observers in aspects of military activity, such as the sharing of secrets and facilities, the military can attempt to reduce the challenging of definitions as journalists feel 'part' of the activities defined. Further, the co-opting of media observers through sharing encourages dramaturgical cooperation with military team members through which military definitions can be generated and sustained. This can be particularly compromising for media observers, potentially undermining their neutrality as reporters. Yet, despite the dangers embedding presents to media objectivity, embedding is often defended within the media fraternity as providing opportunities to gain access to unique war reportage in a manner that does not have to be compromising:

> Embedding is not striking a bargain where poor journalism is inevitable, there is danger that it may happen but it is not inevitable.... There could have been self-censorship, we would have to ask the embeds, but there

seems no evidence in their compromising their journalistic standards with self-censorship. The embeds gave a sense of what fighting a war is like which we did not get in 1991.

(Mark Damazer, Deputy Director of the BBC, 6 May 2003)

In this sense, while cognizant that their objectivity may be compromised, media observers continue to engage in the sharing of secrets and facilities, perhaps because it affords them the opportunity to gain access to what they believe will best meet their institutional needs.

Overall, in the sharing of secrets in interaction with media observers, the military can simultaneously co-opt those who present the greatest danger to their impression management efforts *and* maintain a cover for information they wish to keep concealed. These two key aspects of sharing secrets, as a covering move and uncovering move are important to the effective protection of military definitions from disruption, distortion or discredit. It is noteworthy that while Goffman (1969) makes a distinction between covering moves and counter-uncovering moves, they tend to collapse in the performance of open secrecy and sharing secrets. On the one hand, both are 'covering' in that they are attempting to conceal information. At the same time, and by virtue of their being founded on honest and open engagement, they are also 'counter uncovering', in the sense that they are employed to counteract media suspicion of particular control moves.

In sum, bounded impression management is organized around the assumption that it is in the military's interests to provide information for media observers in order that they can exert control over what is revealed and concealed about their activities. Through the differentiated front and back regions of performances, their engagement in strategic interaction and the regulation of contact that permits more reactive measures such as censorship and denied access, the military attempt to control given patterns of access to information about their activities. While the media may engage in uncovering moves, the boundary definitions of bounded impression management present particular opportunities for the military to define activities in their own terms.

Of course, the success of bounded impression management is contingent on media engagement with the facilities offered. Potential media disillusionment with the military's ability to control and dictate information content and formats can cause the media to look elsewhere for information. In these circumstances, the success of the bounded performance is also contingent on there being no alternative patterns of access to information about the military's activities that might otherwise undermine media reliance on military information, or contradict bounded impression management efforts. With the increasing number of diffuse competitive media outlets, and the rise of independent unilateral journalism, these patterns of access are substantially increased in a manner that can substantially challenge the success of bounded impression management performances.

9 Performing war

Distanciated impression management

In the differentiated front and back regions of co-present bounded impression management, the military are afforded some level of control over the quantity and types of information the media acquire and disseminate about military activities. Beyond these settings, however, control is limited. With increased and amplified patterns of access to information about military activities in the information system, media observers are no longer wholly reliant on the military as an information source. Such increased patterns of access are critical to how the military organize their performances in distanciated impression management. Effective Media Operations are no longer guaranteed through direct, strategic and co-present interaction with media observers alone. Rather, they are determined by the degree to which the military preempt and manage the visibility of their activities in the information system both within and beyond bounded impression management settings. The ways in which the military attempt to do this beyond co-present interaction is the focus of this chapter. The discussion draws and elaborates upon themes previously considered, but also explores the degree to which tactical military actions are increasingly organized around strategic impression management objectives, as all military activity becomes a 'front' in the information system.

In contrast to bounded impression management, distanciated impression management is not bound by co-present interaction with media observers. Instead, the military are required to manage their actions on the assumption that media observers, with whom they have no direct interaction, and among whom there is fervent competition for unique insights, may acquire information about military activity beyond that provided in bounded impression management facilities. Immediacy, co-presence, or place, do not therefore mark the analytical boundaries of distanciated impression management. Rather, in accordance with Meyrowitz's (1985) understanding of the 'information system', distanciated impression management is organized around the degree to which media observers can obtain information about military action through diffuse and diverse patterns of access over which the military have no control. Distanciated impression management is thus characterized by a blurring of the front and back regions, or the cover and the covered.

Given that the definitions communicated through the information system cannot be managed in direct interaction with media observers, distanciated impression management is centrally concerned with distinguishing and managing impressions of activities and events that the military intend to be observed, those they do not intend to be observed and those that are unavoidably observable. As such, distanciated impression management has, what Meyrowitz (1985: 109) terms 'back region bias', in which there is greater likelihood that the back region will be exposed and in which those present are less able to manipulate and control the situation. This notion of 'back region bias' is particularly important to understanding how increased patterns of access have transformed the performance of strategic Media Operations work, *and* the performance of tactical, operational activity. Lastly, although distanciated impression management does not involve co-present interaction, the military still engage in strategic interaction to manage what is acquired and revealed about military activity. In this way, strategic interaction has particular utility in explaining why the tactical and strategic aspects of military activity collapse in distanciated impression management, as control moves become a necessary component of all military activity in order to create 'fronts' for operations and the military institution. The following section considers in more detail the impression management techniques employed for intended observed actions and unavoidably observable actions.

Intended observed actions

Intended observed actions are operational maneuvers executed at a tactical level which, if communicated to audiences via the media, may assist with the generation of favorable impressions and thus belief and action. These intended observed actions are not designed or conducted purely for impression management purposes. Instead, they are planned in accordance with tactical aims and operational objectives. However, in light of the benefits that may accrue if they are communicated via the media, the military consider how best to manage them to maximize their impression management potential. In short, these actions are essentially control moves, undertaken for operational reasons but intentionally organized to generate impressions that will improve the military situation if observed. Examples may include activities like the build-up of troops, the distribution of aid or bombing campaigns. In this manner, the 'shock and awe' bombing of Baghdad was an intended observed action considered by the military to have significantly contributed to their strategic impression management objectives.[1]

In many ways the bombing of Baghdad was unavoidably observable due to its high visibility. Yet, in contrast to those actions that are defined below as 'unavoidably observable', coalition forces *wanted* the bombing to be observed by the media and communicated to audiences to elicit particular responses. For the military, it was considered to spectacularly symbolize the coalition's technological superiority and their commitment to 'liberating' Iraq.[2] In turn, it was hoped that this would simultaneously alleviate potential fears of coalition defeat among external and internal audiences while encouraging capitulation among the adversary audience. As an intended observed action, it was also performed in the knowledge that a large number of journalists were present in Baghdad to observe and communicate it. As such, while the bombing was a key operational maneuver undertaken to advance the military position through the tactical destruction of aspects of the Iraqi regime, it was also a control move performed to strategically generate favorable impressions among audiences.

It remains unclear which of these intentions – tactical or strategic – is considered to reap the greater rewards by the military in terms of operational success. What is clear, however, is that without the tactical action the strategic benefits could not be sought. In this sense, the blurring of tactical and strategic activity in intended observed actions becomes a means through which the military are able to define their activities in a manner that they hope will work to their advantage.

In a similar vein, military activities involving reconstruction and humanitarian work also become intended observed actions. These types of activities are especially beneficial to the military's impression management aims because they allow them to emphasize what they consider to be the more 'liberating' aspects of their work. Hence, during the Iraq War, having (initially) secured Basra, military troops substituted their helmets for berets, organized football matches with the local civilians and began distributing humanitarian aid as part of their intended observed actions.[3] All of these actions are standard tactical and operational maneuvers undertaken to encourage trust, confidence and support for military endeavors among local populations, usually within an Information Operations remit. At the same time, as intended observed actions they have clear strategic benefits if communicated to the external, internal and adversary audiences by defining military action in more progressive and cooperative terms. Moreover, due to the relatively benign environments in which they are performed (usually after the more aggressive aspects of an operation have ended), media observers are able to report on them in a unilateral capacity. The resulting coverage thus appears to be independent of military management and more credible in its neutrality, a fact that further encourages media observation. While, therefore, these actions are not solely staged for the benefit of media observers (in the same manner that press conferences or media facilities are), they are performed in the hope that media observers will be present to observe them.

These examples illustrate how the military attempt to exploit the increased patterns of access to information about their activities through the use of control moves in distanciated impression management. Cognizant of the diminishing capacity to keep operational maneuvers hidden in the information system, they perform specific actions in highly visible ways to actively encourage media observation of them, especially those actions that bolster their defining efforts. More importantly, it is through the use of these control moves that the distinction between tactical activity and strategic impression management is collapsed. Essentially, the military integrate intended observed actions into operational planning on the assumption that they will reap strategic impression management benefits. In their capitalizing on the increased patterns of access to information about their activities, the military thus transform the once private or covered aspects of their activity into a cover or front.

Unavoidably observable actions

In contrast to intended observed actions, there are some actions, executed at a tactical level, that the military anticipate will generate unfavorable impressions but which are inescapably observable due to the lack of military control over access to information about them. These are unavoidably observable actions. These actions usually become unavoidably observable because they are:

1   highly visible operational actions (such as bombing campaigns);
2   unplanned or unintentional actions that become visible and reported upon because they are controversial and newsworthy (such as friendly fire incidents, military casualties);
3   actions that occur within areas where media observers gain access to information beyond Media Operations facilities (including in a unilateral capacity or from adversaries).

These categories are not mutually exclusive. Nor will actions that occur in these categories always be perceived as generating unfavorable impressions. As the previous discussion has highlighted, there are occasions when the military consider unavoidably observable actions to work to their advantage, such as the 'shock and awe' bombing campaign. But the degree to which the action contradicts existing definitions of military activity *and* becomes unavoidably observable can generate substantial concern for the military. To this end, the management of unavoidably observable actions takes two central forms. The first is proactive and the second is defensive.

In a proactive manner, and in the knowledge that some actions become unavoidably observable, the military preempt the unfavorable impressions that an action may generate and organize impression management efforts around this. This, however, is only possible when the action, its observation and response are predicted – or predictable – and where impression management can be organized around this fact. There are certain actions and events that the military consider to be inevitable consequences of war, such as the incurring of casualties, impeded operational progress, friendly fire incidents and equipment failure.[4] During operations it is expected that any, or all, of these actions will become observable at some stage. Owing to the predictable nature of these actions, the military are able to prepare in advance for their eventuality and the possibility that they will become unavoidably observable. One of the ways this is managed is through the dissemination of tacit definitions, usually in bounded impression management facilities. Through this act of revealing information about potentially discreditable scenarios, the military attempt to limit the damage these predictable actions may cause in the future.[5]

Another technique is the use of diversionary tactics. In effect, the military attempt to divert media attention away from a particular incident or action that they wish to keep concealed. This diversion acts as a 'cover'. For example, during the Iraq War, military actions in Az Zubayr were used as a 'cover' for the delay in the securing of Basra. At the time, the military considered the situation in Basra to be too volatile and thus premature for military attack. Concurrently they were conscious that impeded progress in Basra ran contrary to existing definitions emphasizing a speedy resolution to the securing of the region. In their assessment of audience responses to this situation the military were concerned that the delay in Basra would elicit definitions of 'mission creep' in media coverage, which in turn would initiate concern about the overall success of military operations. In this process of imagining these consequences – among both the media and audiences – the military adapted to the possibility of them in an attempt to prevent their occurrence. Consequently, military commanders tried to divert media observers to alternative operations in Az Zubayr in order that their activities could be defined in more progressive and positive terms. As General Reith stated:

> There will be rising pressure from the media saying, 'Why aren't we doing something?' and there will be quite a sort of wobble in the international community as a result. So, we've got to be seen to be achieving some things during that period. What we've got to do is see some progress. So, I think if you [General Robin Brimms], in the next week, can clean up Az Zubayr and get that sorted and then turn the attention. I think that will work perfectly in terms of timings.
>
> (General Reith, *Fighting the War*, BBC 2, June 2003)

Again, this example illustrates the degree to which the military proactively incorporate tactical activity into their performance of strategically oriented distanciated impression management work. With little or no opportunity to impression manage in direct co-present interaction with media observers, the military thus utilize tactical actions to attract (or distract) media attention toward events they *do* want communicated, rather than those they *don't*. Effectively, one form of tactical activity such as the 'cleaning up of Az Zubayr' becomes a 'cover' for predictably disruptive actions elsewhere. In this way the military maximize the impression management potential of intended observed actions to deflect attention away from events that run contrary to their impression management aims.

Of course, the success of proactive tacit definition and diversionary tactics is fundamentally contingent on the degree to which the action is predictable. Yet there will always be military actions or events that are unplanned, unanticipated and unpredictable. For the military, these are unwitting in that they are not oriented toward media observers but may be uncovered by them by virtue of their visibility (Goffman, 1969: 11). Indeed, the military argue that the visibility of unpredicted actions is an inevitable consequence of operations that are performed under the 'ubiquitous' gaze of the media.[6] As such, the uncovering of information by the media comes as no surprise to the military. At the same time, they concede that the intensification of unavoidably observable actions – due to increased patterns of access to information about military activities – has a particularly detrimental effect on their impression management aims.[7] In these situations they are limited to engaging in defensive practices precisely because the unpredictability of the event disallows proactive management. This is the second form of distanciated impression management of unavoidably observable actions. For example, when NATO forces killed a number of Afghan civilians in 2009 during an airstrike in Kunduz, the unpredictability of the action, and the speed with which it was reported, disabled any opportunities to prepare or employ preventative impression management strategies.

In these situations, the military are forced to employ defensive practices to compensate for the discredit brought about by the observed unpredictable action. Typically, this includes the redefining of the situation through either the denial of responsibility or the shifting of discredit. Hence, in response to the NATO airstrike, ISAF (the International Security Assistance Force) spokespeople initially attempted to deny any civilian deaths, claiming instead that those killed were insurgents: 'After observing that only insurgents were in the area, the local ISAF commander ordered air strikes which destroyed the fuel trucks and killed a large number of insurgents' (*Channel 4 News*, 4 September 2009; *BBC News*, 4 September 2009). Eventually, after evidence was uncovered to the contrary, NATO conceded that up to 150 civilians had died as a result of the airstrike. Following this, NATO definitions attempted to shift the discredit to the insurgents. In particular, the culpability of the Taliban was emphasized by virtue of their initial hijacking of the oil tankers and the danger this posed to NATO operations and Afghan 'nation building' (*BBC News*, 4 September 2009). In this way, the construction and incorporation of the Taliban 'threat' to both Afghan civilian lives and the stability of the country became a key (re)defining tool through which the strategic legitimacy of the operation was asserted and sought.

As stated previously, the success of these (re)defining practices and the claims they assert is contingent on the dramaturgical cooperation of all military and political members in the collaborative performance (Goffman, 1959: 88). Yet, the ways in which an action is defined can have largely different consequences for team members (and their respective audience groups), depending on whether they are operating at a tactical and strategic level. Essentially, definitions that may appease, or appeal to, a tactically located audience group will not always placate strategically located audience groups such as the external, home and political audiences.[8] Thus, with reference to the Kunduz airstrike, definitions that attempted to vindicate NATO by stressing the Taliban 'threat' may have mollified the wider diplomatic community but failed to generate the same effect among the Afghan population. Therefore, when President Karzai publicly criticized NATO for needlessly causing the deaths of Afghan civilians, the military argued it was indicative of an individual team member attending to his own tactically focused impression management to the detriment of the overall strategic campaign.[9] Similar examples exist elsewhere. The importance of them, however, resides less in the details of each event than in the degree to which they highlight the challenges of communicating with multiple audiences simultaneously, particularly through the collaborative performance. The military themselves concede that definitions will rarely always appeal to *all* audience groups.[10] But, for the military, these contradictions are brought about by the increased patterns of access to and dissemination of information about their activities beyond their control. While they acknowledge that team members are complicit in the 'uncovering' of tensions between strategic and tactical activity, they attribute this more to the reactive nature with which they have to manage the intense observation of their actions, particularly those that are unpredictable.[11]

In addition, these examples draw attention to standardization of defensive strategies and techniques (discussed in Chapter 7) employed to overcome the challenges that unpredictable, unavoidably observable actions elicit for the military. These are rarely specified in doctrine or in the training of Media Operations personnel. Instead, the dominant focus is on proactive strategies of impression management.[12] In part this is suggestive of how and why unpredictable actions induce defensive responses, not just because the actions themselves are unpredicted, but because scenarios in which they occur are also unimagined and not planned for. Combined, the increased visibility of unpredictable actions and the spontaneity with which the military have to respond affords them few opportunities to impression manage proactively. As a result, they resort to reactive defining, redefining and further redefining in an attempt to counter unfavorable impressions that actions, or alternative definitions of actions may generate. As the strategic and tactical implications implode in this cycle of definitions and counter definitions, so too does the reality of the situation as the act of impression management takes precedence over the incident itself. While the military attribute much of this to operating under the 'ubiquitous' gaze of the media, the following section aims to illustrate how the intense visibility of military action is actually brought about by increased patterns of access generated by both the military *and* the media.

Heightened visibility: the military contribution

While the military highlight that the unavoidably observable nature of actions derives from the diverse and diffuse patterns of access to information about military activities, they rarely engage with their own contribution to this phenomenon. Hence, in their emphasis on the competitive nature of global media outlets, the development of new media outlets and the rise of unilateral reporters, the military appear to disregard the degree to which their own impression management enhances patterns of access by encouraging media observation through intended observed actions and bounded impression management facilities.

First, when the military invite media spectatorship of their actions to promote intended messages, demonstrate credibility and influence the responses of audience groups, they are essentially utilizing the media for their own political and organizational gain. As they state in doctrine, they consider it essential that the military 'seizes the initiative with respect to information, sends clear strategic messages, maintains public confidence and, vitally, is seen as being in control, if not of events then, at the very least, of the UK's response to those events' (JDP 3-45.1, 2007: 1-1). Yet, through their impression management performances they also make public the more private aspects of their operational and tactical work, thereby increasing the potential for unpredictable actions to be observed. For example, during the Iraq War, as a cover for the impeded progress in Basra, they encouraged media observation of their humanitarian aid distribution in Az Zubayr. As a control move, media observance of the aid distribution was considered fundamental to the tactical 'hearts and minds' campaign and simultaneously intended to have strategic influence among the external, political and internal audiences. However, in so doing, they increased the potential for the media to witness unpredictable actions during the distribution. Thus in the ITV coverage of this event it was cited that military personnel appeared unable to retain control of the situation due to civil disturbance and possible militia involvement (*ITV News*, 27 March 2003). ITV correspondent Romilly Weeks stated that the military appeared to be 'struggling to keep control' and that 'order broke down completely as people started to grab boxes of water' (*ITV News*, 27 March 2003). She then claimed that the military were forced to retreat when a local civilian (possibly a member of the militia) fired into the crowd. This coverage ran contrary to both the tactical and strategic impression management objectives that the military had hoped to achieve.

Balancing the risk of unpredictable actions like this against the strategic benefits of intended observed control moves is difficult for the military to achieve when, by their very nature, unpredictable actions are not readily anticipated. Nonetheless, by encouraging media observance of some of their actions, the military fundamentally contribute to the heightened visibility of those unpredictable actions that are detrimental to their strategic objectives. If, as has been suggested earlier, the success of all military impression management is founded on their ability to manage the information made available to media observers, the occurrence of unpredictable actions can profoundly undermine this. It is perhaps for these reasons that a risk-averse military may utilize operational security as a justification or 'cover' for the embargoing of unfavorable media coverage (Bracken, 2009). Certainly, in the example above, Weeks claimed that the military delayed the dispatch of her report for 24 hours, citing 'operational security' as the reason. She believed it was because it was detrimental to their media campaign (*Fighting the War*, BBC 2, June 2003). Of course, this is difficult to ascertain. However, her disclosure does suggest an interplay of strategic interaction moves and counter-moves where the military may have resorted to utilizing the embargoing of material to avoid discredit.

In this sense, the strategies used by the military to perform distanciated impression management are fundamentally related to the degree to which they are able to control the information that is made available to media observers. It is this fluctuating level of control due to increased patterns of access, and their own contribution to these, that determines whether they proactively define their activities through strategic interaction and control moves, or reactively redefine discredited situations or use embargoes. As Figure 9.1 illustrates, this can be mapped on to an axis where the oppositional elements of control and no control, proactive and reactive defining allow us to see more clearly where the different aspects of military media management lie.

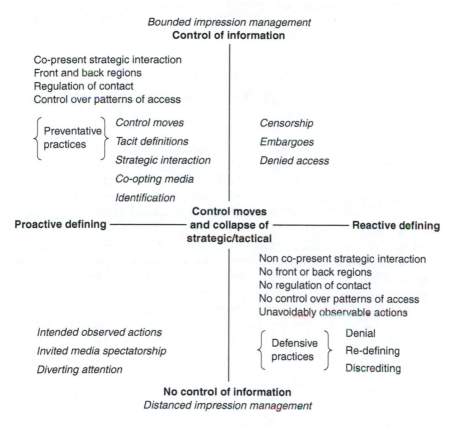

Figure 9.1 Military impression management strategies: defining and performing.

The military often cite the collapse of the conventional distinctions between tactical and strategic actions to be a consequence of media reportage (JDP 3-45.1, 2007: 1-4; see also Badsey, 1994; Peri, 2006). Yet, as has been shown here, there are times when they actively orient their tactical and operational planning to strategic impression management objectives precisely because media observance may reap strategic rewards. This includes the timing of tactical activity to maximize the impression management potential or the incorporation of control and covering moves into operational planning as either intended observed actions or a means of diverting media attention. Hence, in their own attempts to capitalize on the media's observance of their activities, they too blur the distinction of strategic and tactical activity for their own political and organizational gain. In effect, by citing the media as responsible for the damage brought about by the collapse of the tactical and strategic in reportage, the military are actually indicating that there are some tactical actions they would rather were not observed because the impressions they may generate run counter to their overall strategic campaign. Ultimately, in their dependence on the media and the contest of assessment that arises in their strategic interactions with media observers, the military lose autonomy and control over the information disseminated about *all* their activities as a result of their actively promoting *some* of them.

The uncovering perception of media observers

According to the military, during the Iraq War there were a number of unpredictable actions that they knew little about until they were communicated through the media.[13] Examples cited included the downing of an Apache helicopter, the capture of British prisoners of war and the ambush and killing of two British soldiers, established through Al Jazeera broadcasts. In this later example, while the soldiers were known to be missing in action, it was only through the Al Jazeera report that the military were able to confirm they had been killed.[14] They stated that this was not the first time they had learned about casualties through media reportage. Indeed, they had expected that during the Iraq War coalition deaths would receive intense media attention, particularly because it was anticipated that the number of deaths would be relatively low.[15] Nonetheless, the Al Jazeera report demonstrated to the military how media observers were increasingly able to acquire information about tactical events from alternative sources that undermined reliance on official military definitions, and in a manner that was relatively unique at the time.[16] Moreover, once broadcast on Al Jazeera, these same reports were subsequently syndicated to various other media outlets. For the British military, it was particularly notable that these reports were reproduced on all major British terrestrial television channels (see *BBC 1 News*, *ITV News*, *Channel 4 News*, 25–26 March 2003). Not only did this demonstrate the multiplicity of information sources, but also the multiplicity of media distributors that could duplicate the same coverage globally.

It is well recognized that the media can draw upon diffuse and diverse sources of information about conflict scenarios, not least because each party to a conflict, including adversaries, civilians and even military members, realize the potential utility of the media for their own political gain (Cottle, 2006). For the military, however, the example above was evidence of the increasing uncovering perception of media observers and the ways in which this might impact upon their impression management work. With the rise in unilateral journalism, coupled with advances in media technologies, the media's 'perception abilities' have been further enhanced. Moreover, these have been fuelled by increasing competition between global media outlets that have generated an ongoing demand for new information about, and unique insights into, military activities beyond those the military provide themselves.

The heightened uncovering perception of media observers does not simply derive from the competition between media organizations, however. The degree to which media observers are able to 'uncover' the military 'cover' is also fundamentally related to their involvement in the complex symbiotic relationship with major political actors such as the military. In the contest of assessment that shapes and is shaped by the strategic interactions of both parties, the media will use information to try to expose possible political manipulation relative to their own position. With the increasing development of what Edelmen (1964) first recognized as 'symbolic politics', journalists are now all too aware of the dramaturgical aspects of military media management and the compromising role this can place them in. The penetration of military staging thus becomes a means through which they can resist this role and assert their own independence. Unpredictable actions provide an ideal platform for such endeavors. With little room for military concealment, the media seize upon these events to reveal the potential inauthenticity of supposedly authentic military performances, and in a manner from which they stand to gain themselves. The uncovering perception of media observers is thus about resistance as much as it is about competition (Swanson, 1997). Needless to say, this resistance is made relative to the environment in which it is enacted. However, it is in the contestation – albeit symbiotic – that exists between the military and the media, and through these attempts to 'uncover' information that the media also contribute to the obscuring of reality in the compromising of their own partisanship (see also Mazzoleni and Schulz, 1999).

In sum, the notion of distanciated impression management allows us to draw together the various strands of military media management discussed in previous chapters. As a result, the use of specific defining techniques, and the ways in which they are performed through control moves and strategic interaction with media observers, have been shown to be as relevant for non-co-present impression management as co-present impression management. The key difference with distanciated impression management, however, and predicated on the military's limited ability to control the types of information the media acquire, is that it is characterized by the military's attempts to capitalize on the visibility of their actions, or to manage the exposure of actions that may be detrimental to their overall aims. In this way, and as a result of its 'back region bias', distanciated impression management allows us to better understand how the collapse of strategic and tactical actions results from the actions of both military *and* the media as each party attempts to fulfill their own respective institutional and impression management needs.

10 Mediatized war and impression management
Negotiating the 'front' line

It was in 1991 that Jean Baudrillard first proclaimed that the Gulf War did not take place (see also Baudrillard, 1995). This was not, of course, a denial of the physical and social reality of the Gulf War. A war did take place. Lives were lost and victories were claimed. But for Baudrillard the significance of this war lay in its imploded reality, in which the symbolic world of the mediated war assumed such dominance that it became more real than reality. Baudrillard concluded that our perceptions and understandings of this war, and our relation to it, were so fundamentally steered by media representation that it was hyperreal. Wars were no longer what they once were. For many, this implosion of fact and fiction, reality and mediated reality was distinctly postmodern and indicative of the mediatization of our social world beyond (but including) conflict scenarios (Cummings, 1992; Kellner, 1992; Baudrillard, 1993a; Brown, 1993; Virillio, 1994). For others, the dissolution of distinctions between reality and mediated reality, fact and fiction – as articulated in the postmodern conceptualization of mediatization – are at once too simple and too grand. Hjarvard (2008a), for instance, argues that rather than collapsing, these distinctions remain but have been profoundly altered by the processes of mediatization and media intervention. Reality has not therefore been supplanted by mediated reality, but rather there are differentiations in what people perceive to be real.

The discrepancies in these quite different interpretations of mediatization – postmodern and institutional, respectively – are symptomatic of the degree to which academics are still grappling with competing frameworks through which to understand it (Väliverronen, 2001; Livingstone, 2009b). While some employ the term 'mediatization' to describe different phenomena, others describe the same phenomena but variously term it mediazation, mediation, medialization or mediatization (Thompson, 1995; Silverstone, 2005; Livingstone, 2009a; Hjarvard, 2008a). Perhaps it is due to these conceptual ambiguities that 'mediatization' has been used to describe a myriad of interdependent war and media practices, but with little theoretical and empirical clarification regarding how they are 'mediatizing' (Livingstone, 2009a; McQuail, 2006). To avoid these same pitfalls, the following discussion offers some clarity with regard to how 'mediatization' is conceptualized and applied here.

Impression management and mediatized war

Conceivably, the clearest articulation of 'mediatization' as a concept, and one that is applicable to the work contained within this book, is to be found in Hjarvard's work (2004, 2007, 2008a, 2008b). For Hjarvard, mediatization is the degree to which society is increasingly submitted to, and dependent upon, the media and their logic (2008a: 113). The intensification and changing importance of the media in society has thus led to institutions – including politics, family, religion and in this case the military – integrating the media into their operations. In other words, the activities of these institutions are increasingly performed through the media. At the same time, the media have also acquired the status of a social institution *in their own right* with a logic of their own that other social institutions have to accommodate. As a consequence, social interaction – within institutions, between institutions and in society at large – takes place via the media. What Hjarvard means by this is that the media constitute an interface through which institutions communicate with each other and their publics (Hjarvard, 2008a: 125). This is more than mediation, however. While mediation is the act of communication through a medium, mediatization is when the institutions and their modes of interaction have been changed as a consequence of the growth of media influence.

According to Hjarvard, the processes of mediatization are also characterized by duality. This is important because it recognizes that the ways mediatization affects and shapes society are not uni-directional or technologically determined (inherent in some theorization of mediatization). As such, Hjarvard distinguishes between direct and indirect forms of mediatization (Hjarvard, 2004; 2008a: 115). In direct mediatization, formerly non-mediated activity converts to a mediated form. He offers the example of online chess and online banking, which were formerly reliant on direct interaction and have changed the behavior of all those involved by the expanded opportunities that 'online' engagement provides. Indirect mediatization, however, is when the media and the symbolic world of the media increasingly influence an existing activity. Again, the example he provides is a visit to McDonald's, where, in the process of obtaining a meal, one is also exposed to a cultural context surrounding the eating experience – particularly the opportunity to collect or purchase merchandise from current films and cartoons. Crucially, it is often hard to distinguish between direct and indirect forms of mediatization because they will often operate in combination (Hjarvard, 2008a). Attempts to do so, however, may better elucidate the strength of the media influence or mediatization processes that are transforming the institutions concerned.

This conceptualization of mediatization is not only intelligible, but has particular utility here because its institutional approach allows for an analysis of the interplay between the institutions of the media, the military and their publics. In addition, Hjarvard's definition reduces aspects of mediatization to concrete processes that can be analyzed empirically (Lundby, 2009). Indeed, both Krotz (2007) and Hjarvard (2008a) identify that empirical studies of mediatization processes – in specific contexts and among different groups – are necessary if the concept is to be useful (see also Hjarvard, 2004, 2007, 2008b). This book is an attempt to do just this; to analyze the processes by which the military (and the wars they conduct) are interdependent – that is, 'mediatized'.

To this end, Goffman's (1959, 1969) theories of impression management and strategic interaction were employed as conceptual tools through which mediatizing processes, particularly military interaction with – and organization of action around – the media, could be made more explicit. It has been argued that acts of war, and the ways in which they are reported, are ultimately impression management performances, constructed for audiences in a manner that attempts to advance each institution's respective causes. The mediatization of war conduct and its reportage can thus be understood as resulting from the activities of, and interactions between, *both* the military and the media. This allows us to see more clearly *how* and *why* the practice of war is mediatized; that is, enacted through, involves and is dependent upon the media. In order to clarify and expand upon this, the following discussion revisits the central findings of this book and the implications regarding how the relationship between war and media may be constituted within Hjarvard's mediatization concept.

Media logic, military logic

It is well recognized that official institutions are increasingly willing to engage with the media to achieve political and organizational ends and protect against vulnerabilities (see, for example, Gitlin, 1980; Ericson *et al.*, 1989; Schlesinger and Tumber, 1994; Swanson and Mancini, 1996; Mazzoleni and Schulz, 1999; Manning, 2003). So, too, are the military. In recognition of the strategic and tactical importance of media involvement, the military have progressively incorporated media management into their activities. It is here that the processes of mediatization become more evident as the military institution – and war conduct – is transformed by a progressive dependence upon, and integration of the media into operational planning. In short, militaries recognize that the execution of war increasingly has an intrinsic 'performance' element, and therefore consciously and purposefully organize their activities to coincide with those of media organizations (see also Molotch and Lester, 1974).

Inherent within this mediatizing process is the logic of the media through which military activities assume media form (Altheide and Snow, 1979). Media logic thus becomes an implicit orientation framework that guides and influences the content, structure and organization of military action in a manner that conforms to media production (see Schrott, 2009; Mazzoleni, 2008a). Indeed, it is during the ongoing process of 'properties of play' – wherein the military take account of other's real and anticipated actions and the bearing of that response on their own future actions (Goffman, 1969; see also Mead, 1967) – that media logic can be seen to take effect. The military organize their actions and impression management performances on the basis of what they believe will best appeal to the media *and* media audiences. Consequently, performances are shaped by the conventional and dominant values of the logic of the media and the grammar of mediated communication, especially simplification, drama and narrative form. Strategic and tactical performances incorporate visual imperatives, transformative narratives and symbolically laden catchphrases. Media logic is therefore fundamental to the construction of the impression management performance because it offers a means through which the military can secure the communication of the performance to mass audiences in an attempt to influence, in their favor, audience responses. The more dependent militaries are on media audiences for support for their activities, the more this logic will shape and reshape their actions (see Doyle, 2003).

Crucially, however, as Hjarvard (2008a) stresses, the media do not merely function as 'mediators' in this regard. Rather, the military institution and its activities are transformed as a result of their orientation to media logic because it is the primary means through which the military can elicit support and legitimatization. Consequently, it has fundamentally altered the ways in which they structure, organize and communicate their activities beyond those intended for mass mediation. With a diminishing capacity to conceal their actions from what they call the 'ubiquitous' media gaze, the military have adapted their institutional practices to accommodate their potential visibility. Most notably, they now orient and construct aspects of tactical activity in accordance with strategic impression management objectives, collapsing the distinction between tactical and strategic action in the process. Examples cited here include the timing of tactical activity in a manner that will capitalize on the strategic impression management potential, or the conscious organization of tactical action for strategic purposes such as the diversion of media attention from activity they would prefer not to have reported on. The increasing 'performance' element in these tactical activities is illustrative of how *all* military activity is assuming a media form as it becomes an institutional and political 'front'.

At the same time, it is clear that the media also orient themselves to and rely upon official sources in order to guarantee regular supplies of information (Chibnall, 1977; Hall *et al.*, 1978; Fishman, 1980; Ericson *et al.*, 1991; Schlesinger and Tumber, 1994). While the military do not constitute the only source of information, they still remain a dominant source, particularly in light of the dangers in war zones that can inhibit a search for alternative, verifiable information (see Tumber, 2003; Taylor, 1996; Gowing, 1996b; Burns, 1996). Under these conditions the media can become dependent on militaries for information, be they regular or irregular. Cognizant of this, and by virtue of their authoritative status as providers of primary definitions of situations, the military can harness the media for their own legitimation purposes. They can, for example, dictate the situations that come to be reported, produce 'authorized' definitions of situations, and exert power through the censoring of reportage. The media remain at the behest of these processes when utilizing the military as a primary information source, allowing the military better control over the consequences of the communications (see Doyle, 2003).

Consequently, while media logic influences the organization of military action, so too can military actions have a distinct influence on the organization of the media according to the logic of the military. With intense international competition for news promotion, accelerated by the growth of satellite television and the compression of time and space, the media are driven by a persistent search for information that is both exclusive and fits with audience demand. In this sense, they too are engaged in impression management – performed through their reportage of war – as a means through which to secure audience retention and market share. As a result, media observers orient themselves and their actions to fit with military practice in order to produce reportage about war situations for their own institutional purposes. This orientation to 'military logic' is perhaps most apparent in the correlations between the increasing number of spectacular maneuvers in military planning and a disproportionate media focus on such events (Shaw, 1996; Gowing, 1996a). Similarly, it helps explain the degree to which the media continue to embed with military units despite the narrow perspective these opportunities can offer and the potential compromising of media objectivity (Tumber and Palmer, 2004; Morrison, 1994; Morrison and Tumber, 1988). Put simply, there are influences exerted on the media that largely take place within parameters set by the military and through which the military attempt to establish power and authority over the circulated definitions of their activities.

Predicated on these respective logics, mediatization and the transformations inherent within its processes become consequences of the institutional actions of *both* the military and the media. Their relationship is at once reciprocal and resistant, informed by and responding to the conditions in which it is enacted – including an orientation to their respective logics – as each attempts to meet their particular impression management and institutional needs. Moreover, their actions are mutually reinforcing and cyclical, giving us an indication of how both parties contribute to the mediatized war environment. On the one hand, there is nothing new in this claim. Others have highlighted how the interdependence of war and media is intrinsically founded on the relationship between the military and the media (Cottle, 2006, 2008; Hoskins, 2004; Hoskins and O'Loughlin, 2010). Within these analyses there is ample recognition that the media are cognizant that their reportage is, to a large extent, a shaping mechanism in the conduct of war. Similarly, there is an appreciation of how the military orient themselves to the media for legitimation purposes. On the other hand, however, few authors elucidate the manner through which these effects and transformations come about, particularly with regard to military practice. Hence, in Hoskins and O'Loughlin's (2010: 19) analysis of mediatized war, questions remain regarding how militaries design war for the media and how the media is designed for war. In part, these questions are answerable through the analysis of the 'logics' that each bring to bear on their own institutional practice. In addition, however, by viewing the military–media relationship as a product of social relations, where both are engaged in strategic interaction alongside an orientation to their logics, mediatizing processes can be made more explicit.

Strategic interaction

Goffman's (1969) notion of strategic information management has been utilized here to describe the processes by which the military and media strategically manage information in interaction with each other in an attempt to acquire, reveal and conceal information about their own and others' activities. While it is in the interests of the media to acquire information about the military, it is simultaneously in the interests of the military to appreciate that this is occurring and to control and manage the information that the media obtain. In situations where the media are dependent on the information provided by the military – there being no sufficient alternate sources of information – a contest of assessment develops. In this contest, the military engage in a sequence of moves, counter-moves and adaptations in an attempt to court and influence, in their favor, media and audience responses. Similarly, the media attempt to glean information from the military from which they stand to gain while simultaneously trying to expose possible military manipulation relative to their own position.

In the resulting strategic interaction the complex symbiotic relationship between the media and military creates a dynamic of cooperation and competition, manipulation and resistance. For example, in the strategic interaction that occurs between military subjects and media observers, the military employ linguistic and visual control moves to account for and explain their operational activity in a manner that is both favorable to them and submits to the logic of the media to secure their communication. Essentially, the military set the stage beforehand in a self-conscious and calculated manner so as to improve their own situation. Similarly, 'covering' moves are intentionally produced to conceal information that may generate unfavorable impressions. But, in the use of control moves, an environment is created in which media observers will seek to uncover what is being obscured in accordance with their own institutional requirements that demand impartiality, neutrality, objectivity and exclusivity. The media thereby seek out information that seems immune to military fabrication and management. Essentially, the performance, or suspected performance, of military 'control moves' or 'covering moves' generates conditions in which the media employ 'uncovering moves' to penetrate the 'staging' of the definition and uncover what is being concealed or obscured. Similarly, the performance, or suspected performance, of media 'uncovering moves' – whether in response to control moves or not – generates conditions in which the military engage in further 'control moves', 'covering moves' or 'counter-uncovering moves', to give media observers a false sense of advantage or suppress their misgivings. This process is not linear but variable and fluid, based upon the initial move by either the media or the military. The resulting strategic information management is increasingly complex as moves become subject to constant development through this interactive process and reality becomes embedded in and through the media.

Lastly, and of critical importance, is the degree to which these interaction processes involve multiple 'players'. Conflict, by its very nature, involves at least two military forces. Media observers, in accordance with their own aims, will rarely position themselves in relation to just one. In these circumstances, the 'contest of assessment' extends beyond interaction between *a* military subject and media observer(s) to include the strategies of both, or *all* warring factions party to a conflict. What develops is a complex interplay between militaries and the media, who are mutually aware of each others' involvement and whose moves and counter-moves are founded on a continual assessment of the consequences of their actions for themselves and others.

This symbolic interactionist perspective has particular utility in furthering our understanding of the interdependence between war and media as a product of social relations between those conducting war and those reporting war. The result is mediatized war, in which the substantive elements of war actions become inseparable from the ways in which they are defined and performed for impression management purposes, and in which the practice of war is submitted to and dependent upon the media. The notion that military information management involves censorship and secrecy is not precluded by this framework of understanding, nor is Badsey's (1994) alternative proposition that the military–media relationship is founded on cooperation and an open information policy. Yet phrases like 'perception management' inadequately express the complexities of these interactions, not least because they are predominantly associated with military information management – or control – and fail to acknowledge the ability of the media to disrupt and destabilize military planning. Strategic interaction, however, incorporates all of these possibilities. Indeed, in contrast to dichotomized and simplistic control versus cooperation formulations, it indicates how the relationship between the military and the media incorporates all the above formulations when both parties negotiate the contest of assessment for their own respective ends. Hence, it is in the contest of assessment that mediatized war can be seen to shape, and be shaped by the proactive and reactive actions of both the military and the media in interaction with each other.

The active imagined audience

Lastly, the impression management framework acknowledges and clarifies the significance of audiences to military media management and mediatized war. As has been shown here, the military conceptualize their impression management audiences as distinct, differentiated groups, each of whom can significantly determine the organization of impression management performances. The following discussion explores this in more detail, moving away from the recognized difficulties of attempting to show the influence of media on audiences, and instead considering the relatively unexplored area of potential audience influence on the organization of action (see Doyle, 2003).

At this stage it is important to remember that the military's engagement in impression management is founded on their desire to achieve influence. Performances are constructed so as to encourage or persuade 'others' to act in accordance with military objectives and organizational goals. To this end, the media are the means through which performances are disseminated; the audience is the intended recipient. It is thus with audiences in mind that the military coherently, and collectively, define their activities for the media for it is among audiences that they hope impressions will be formed, legitimation sought and persuasion enacted. However, the military must first conceive of a sense of audience, among whom responses to impression management performances will be manifest, in order to know best how to construct the performance to achieve influence. They are able to do this by taking the role of the audience and interrogating their actions from the point of view of the audience to gauge how their actions may be perceived and understood (Goffman, 1959; Mead, 1967). Those whose potential responses have a significant impact upon the military's political, institutional, strategic and tactical activities thereby come to be identified as the audience with whom the military most wish to communicate. Through this process the military identify various audience groups upon whom they rely for legitimation or resources: the political audience who govern the military institution and essentially dictate the 'working' environments in which the military operate; the internal audience who are critical to the maintenance of morale among military personnel; the adversary audience, whose responses can potentially lead to capitulation or prolonged battle; and the domestic audience, whose support is perceived as having a direct impact on the responses of the other audiences.

Despite the identification of these groups, however, and in light of the distanciated relationship the military have with their audience, it is inherently difficult for them to ascertain, with any certainty, who their audiences *actually* comprise. Instead, based on the limited amount of information available, they construct an essentially 'imagined audience' – in accordance with the categories outlined above. Similarly, the military are also unable to gauge the degree to which the imagined audience *actually* observe and respond to performances communicated via the media. Consequently, performances are fundamentally organized around a *potential* for audience observation rather than a manifest and clear indication that this actually occurs. Lastly, devoid of an accurate means with which to measure audience responses, the military make assumptions about what responses may be provoked by viewing themselves from the perspective of the audience. These assumptions then become critical to the design and formation of the performance itself. From this, there lies an implicit presumption that the desired audience response will be elicited if the media report on the performance in the manner in which it was intended by the military. Of course, in reality, this circumnavigates the way audiences may actually perceive, interpret and respond to military performances. But, for the military, with few other means to measure the success of a performance among audiences, the media coverage becomes the measurement. This is a further 'imagining' of audience responses based on indicators constructed from the media coverage itself.

All of these factors culminate in series of unknowns, particularly with regard to how audience members may respond. As a result of their 'imaginings' the military conceive of and anticipate numerous possibilities, over which they cannot be certain but around which they organize the performance. Audiences thereby become critically implicated in how the military formulate their actions and interactions with the media. Essentially, the construction of the performance is at once submitted to media logic *and* potential audience responses.

Coupled with this, there is the consistent possibility that the more 'private' aspects of their operational work will be exposed and made available to audiences via the media. This potential increasingly requires the military to take the role of the 'imagined audience' in the formulation of *all* their actions and strategic interactions in order to protect against the undermining of their impression management efforts. Consequently, the role of the audience is no longer limited to spectator, but in fact constitutes an additional – and key – participant in the strategic interaction between the military and the media. Although the 'imagined audience' have little, if any, direct engagement in strategic moves, the potential for them to observe military performances introduces them into the situations defined. Of course, this does not necessarily create a vehicle for active involvement. But, neither should it be understood as entirely passive. Instead, the audience (and their potential to observe and respond) constitutes a powerful influence in the strategic interaction between militaries and media as actions, moves and counter-moves are intrinsically organized around assumptions about how the final media product will be perceived and understood by audiences. This changes the meaning of the situation for all involved. It alters the behavior of the various participants, necessitating them to take the role of the 'imagined audience(s)' and their anticipated responses in the organization of their actions. It is through these processes that war is evidentially mediatized as social interaction – both within and beyond the military and media institutions – increasingly takes place via the media.

Negotiating the 'front' line: unknown unknowns

Distinctions between the ways in which war is conducted and the ways in which it is reported have increasingly collapsed in the twenty-first century. War is no longer an activity that takes place outside of the media. Rather, the media have become progressively integrated into the planning and organization of war as a weapon of persuasion and a legitimation tool. In part, these conditions have been influenced by the processes of globalization, in which activities between states increasingly involve the interconnectedness, interdependence and reciprocity required for the organization, coordination and planning of activities on a global scale (Thompson, 1995). The growing need to preserve economic, political and diplomatic alliances on which the global economy depends has particular significance for the conduct of war. With the advance of global alliances there has been a declining propensity for dominant Western nations to go to war for territorial reasons. Indeed, threats to states are no longer defined by or limited to geographic boundaries because of the increasing global infrastructure. Instead, wars now tend to be fought on the principles of preserving alliances and specific ideologies, a strategy of containment in Wight's (1979) terms. The need for preservation requires states to explain and validate their war actions on a global scale and in accordance with the transnational social, political and legal norms that bind them with other reciprocal states. This necessitates states (and their militaries) to draw upon and respond to media reportage to justify political decisions, display political might or formulate alliances where previously there were none. Simultaneously, those excluded from global alliances engage in the same processes to generate a political presence that would otherwise be denied. As such, the media becomes a pivotal source and resource through which those involved in war can interact, plan and communicate their war actions in a manner that may permit political leverage.

Coupled with this, the proliferation of media industries and technologies, and their predominant independence from state control has spawned an environment of global media scrutiny in which the actions of those involved in war, and the consequences of those actions, are open to view on a mass public scale. In recognition of this, and in the knowledge that the media can be harnessed for political outcomes, all those involved in war – including militaries, insurgent forces and civilians – attempt to mobilize the media in order to generate or sustain power. Correspondingly, attempts to contradict or undermine information in the media become as prolific as attempts to promote particular types of information. The media thus becomes a shared arena in which all those involved in the conduct of war compete to define their activities in a manner from which they will profit. As a result, the media not only provides the context in which war is performed, it also has a distinct influence on *how* it is performed due to the increasing potential for all actions to fall under the mass public gaze. The consequence of all of these factors is that war has become mediatized, where its practice is enacted through and dependent upon the media, from the strategic and political justification to the tactical ways in which it is actually conducted.

Some would argue that this trend is reflective of the need of militaries to adapt to changes outside of the military structure, particularly in the media environment (see Janowitz, 1971; Moskos, 1992; Badsey, 1996, 2001). Indeed, this was the dominant attitude among military personnel in this research. Yet, given the marginalization of kinetic force, the centrality of strategic and tactical influencing activities in the conduct of contemporary warfare is not simply a response to an external 'media' world; it is an indication of how the military institution proactively contributes to the mediatization of war. Thus, while the military do not create mediatization, changes in their practices have enhanced the conditions under which war has become mediatized. Their increasing emphasis on 'influencing activities' in asymmetric wars like Afghanistan, for instance, is particularly demonstrative of how the media have become instrumental in, and fundamental to, military practice precisely because kinetic superiority no longer guarantees 'winning' (Maltby, 2010).

However, influencing activities are not limited to a theater of operations, as traditional conceptualizations of asymmetric and guerilla warfare would contend, where local populations – through intimidation or reward – provide the 'sea in which the fish can swim' (Laqueur, 1977). Rather, influencing activity has adapted to the conditions in which it is now being conducted where, due to increasing reliance on strategic global alliance networks, influencing is also intended to act upon strategic audiences. We see this with NATO and the United Nations, whose partners are geographically dispersed but simultaneously united in the common goals of the alliance because of its strategic importance to each individual partner.

Generating and sustaining the cooperation and collaboration of partners is critical to each partner, the alliance they inhabit and the activities they engage in. For instance, conflict withdrawal by a NATO partner could be catastrophic for those partners that remain. The same could also be said of networks like Al Qaeda, who appear to be – or are certainly constructed as – a globalized alliance of partners who, reliant on the reciprocity of other globally connected groups and the power that the collective generates, become unified under the collective umbrella of 'jihad'. This simultaneous engagement in asymmetric warfare and the protection of global alliances has thus necessitated that influence activity – for all those engaged in the conflict – must extend beyond the tactical audience to include the strategic audience if militaries are to mobilize the support necessary for the continuation of power. Again, this is not simply a response to the growth of media influence. Rather, it is military strategy, which, at its core, is attempting to affect change in the same manner as traditional weaponry or political diplomacy. In short, it is a mode of warfare that has developed from – and because of – conditions that exist beyond the media.

At the same time, the techniques and strategies used to achieve influence have been enhanced and transformed by the growth of media influence. In this sense, mediatized war is at once a direct and indirect form of mediatization in Hjarvard's terms, and indicative of how both forms operate in combination and become difficult to distinguish (Hjarvard, 2008a: 115). Put simply, the media have not generated the conditions for military influencing activities, but the form and organization of influencing activity increasingly submits to and is dependent upon the media. For example, both NATO and the Taliban now utilize social networking sites and SMS messaging as vehicles of influence, particularly among tactical populations. In this way, non-mediated activity and interactions have assumed a mediated form because of the influencing opportunities that these media technologies offer. Similarly, in the knowledge that they cannot circumvent the intrinsic compression of space, time and information flows inherent in media practice, militaries have attempted to harness the opportunities this presents by adapting their war strategies to the point where 'influence pervades everything they do'; war *is* the battle for influence. To this end, they engage in impression management and strategic interaction as a means through which to generate this influence. In this way, militaries are not just responding and adapting to the media, but proactively contributing to the construction of the environment in which mediatized war is enacted.

Under these conditions, impression management becomes a useful framework to understand and interrogate the strategies of numerous warring factions wishing to generate a political presence. Essentially, through the media, rhetoric, protestations and demonstrable acts of war become means through which to attain influence. The conscious and calculated use of control moves to galvanize attention and generate influence is therefore apparent in the 'performances' of regular militaries, irregular militaries and terrorist organizations alike. The videoing of the Moscow Theatre and Beslan school sieges by Chechen Rebels; the videoing of the beheading of hostages by terrorist organizations such as Tawhid Wal Jihad;[1] the videoing of detonated IEDs by insurgent groups in Iraq; all of these abhorrent acts of violence have within them an inherent media logic that suggests they are organized around their impression management potential to influence the responses of others. They are forms of symbolic communication as much as they are forms of extreme violence (Schmid and DeGraaf, 1982; Paletz and Schmid, 1992; Baudrillard, 1993b; Juergensmeyer, 2000; Tuman, 2003). Essentially, they are impression management performances through which legitimacy and powerful alliances are sought (relative to each militaries' position).

For the media, the observation, interpretation and distribution of these 'performances' allows them to also define themselves and their organizations in accordance with their own objectives. Thus, militarist performances, in turn, feed back into the organization of action and interaction, between and through the media. What ensues is a competition over definitions *in* the media, and a complex interplay between militaries (and media organizations) *through* the media where each party is mutually aware of their own and others' performances, continually assessing others' actions in relation to their own.

Concurrently, there are also those devoid of political power who try to render themselves and their circumstances visible through the media in an attempt to harness power or challenge existing power relations. When, for example, human-rights activist, Taher Thabet al-Hadithi filmed the dead bodies of Iraqis in Haditha in 2005, it was with the intent to expose the massacring of 24 innocent civilians by US soldiers (see *Time Magazine*, 19 March 2006). Indeed, elsewhere, media reports suggest that victims of conflicts are increasingly prepared to film war atrocities committed against their fellow community members in the hope that, when disseminated in the global media, political intervention or justice may result.[2] Inherent in all these examples is the understanding, or assumption, that a media presence can offer empowerment. Consequently, even the victims of war alter their behaviors in mediatized war; they too engage in the filming, recording and distribution of information about war events in the hope that it may diminish their isolation and enhance the potential to demand political change. What results is what has been described here as increased patterns of access to information about others (Meyrowtiz, 1985). These patterns are diverse and diffuse, generated and sustained by all those seeking empowerment, a political presence and legitimation, including the media themselves.

The greater significance of these access patterns, however, is that they fundamentally diminish the opportunities for all parties to a conflict to conceal information. The once private, back region work of militaries has the potential to become public at any point. The Haditha massacre is a key example of such a phenomenon. In response, as has been shown here, militaries attempt to anticipate and accommodate these contingencies by incorporating 'performance elements' into the organization and execution of their actions. War, in this sense, is performed, staged and enacted to achieve influence. But, there are some incidents that militaries are unable to anticipate. Equally, they are also unable to anticipate where, how and when information about their private activities may materialize. Again, Haditha is a poignant example, but so too was the exposure of atrocities in Abu Ghraib in 2006, or Kevin Site's film of the killing of an injured Iraqi fighter in Fallujah in 2004. All of them highlight the degree to which the emergence of 'private' actions is unpredictable and unknowable in mediatized war. Hoskins and O'Loughlin term this condition 'Diffuse War' where the relationship between cause and effect is diffuse and where militaries (and policy makers) must learn to manage ambiguity and unexpected feedback: 'diffused war requires learning, adaptation and managing feedback, and not a fixed doctrine. The result is permanent war against contingency itself, a diffused war without end' (Hoskins and O'Loughlin, 2010: 12). Indeed, despite being ridiculed for impenetrable articulation, Donald Rumsfeld captured the sentiment behind this concept of Diffused War in his (now) infamous statement about the complexities of knowing:

> there are known knowns; there are things we know we know. We also know there are known unknowns; that is to say we know there are some things we do not know. But there are also unknown unknowns; the ones we don't know we don't know … it is the latter category that tend to be the difficult ones.
>
> (Secretary of Defense Donald Rumsfeld, Department of Defense News Briefing, 12 February 2002)

It is within this context of unknown unknowns that militaries attempt to shape *all* of their actions for the media. Impression management becomes so pervasive that *all* military activity is organized in a manner so as to act as a 'front'. This does not, of course, protect against the risks of exposure, but as the Rumsfeld quote suggests, it does indicate the degree to which militaries increasingly recognize, and attempt to structure their actions around, the potential for unforeseen contingencies. What is less apparent in Rumsfeld's quote, however, is the degree to which militaries themselves contribute to the potential visibility of their more 'private' works by encouraging media spectatorship. Indeed, in contrast, here it has been suggested that the military understand contingencies to be 'things' that happen to them rather than something to which they contribute, in an environment of which they are part. Thus despite their reliance on the media, there still remains a traditional reticence toward media engagement, which further adds to the desire to protect and hide particular actions. Of course, this is rarely acknowledged publicly but may be a factor in the loss of political and military autonomy over certain types of information. In short, by actively promoting some of their activities, they expose themselves to contingencies and the potential disclosure of 'private' activities.

Ultimately, it is by virtue of all these practices, including the unpredictable and unknowable qualities of mediatized war that we, as vicarious participants, come to know about the actions of others in conflict. Perhaps it is for these reasons that Meyrowitz (1985: 132) suggests the availability and communicability of information in the information system is indirectly liberating, undermining hierarchy and the segregation of knowledge. Of course, the authenticity of this information is at times questionable as the reality of war becomes increasingly elusive in the competition over, and interactions between, militarist performances and the media. Yet, as Hjarvard (2008a) suggests, reality is not supplanted by, or imploded into, a media reality. Tangible acts of war – and violence – still remain, which emerge in the media and enact upon us and all those involved in the execution of war, including militaries. It is through the visibility of these acts that those involved can be held to account. Thus, although there are problematic aspects regarding the growing influence of the media and its logic on the conduct of war, it is not necessarily synonymous with a decline in the political public sphere (Hjarvard, 2008a; see also Mazzoleni and Schulz, 1999). Rather, it is precisely because the implications of mediatized war can be so great that we need to better understand the empirical reality for those engaged in it. Goffman's dramaturgical perspective, with its orientation to revealing implicit knowledge in interaction; with its emphasis on the symbolic value of what is said and done; and with its focus on the production and reproduction of action through social relations, allows us to do this. Offering a conceptual toolkit, Goffman enables us to better understand how militaries understand and organize war in these times of mediatization.

Notes

1 Introduction

1 Goffman is frequently characterized as a leading exponent of symbolic interactionism. For example, Scheff (2005) argues that for most of his career, Goffman was a symbolic interactionist in the Cooley line of the 'looking glass self'. Goffman was certainly 'sympathetic' to Herbert Blumer, the founder of symbolic interactionism, and his writings on concepts and methods (Verhoeven, 1993: 320). However, as Goffman himself observed in interview, symbolic interactionism was too vague a characterization of social life to provide his sociology with much guidance (Smith, 2006: 31). Here, Goffman's approach is considered to resonate with the symbolic interactionist perspective enough for it to be justifiable to label him one.

2 The college was originally established in 1997 in order to provide opportunities for all British military services – Navy, Airforce and Army – to develop a common understanding of warfare and defense approaches. It provides command and staff training at junior, advanced and higher levels for servicemen and MoD civilians.

2 What are Media Operations?

1 Source: military document: Joint Media Handling Guide, Draft 4.0.

2 Source: ethnographic fieldwork with the British military in May 2003; military document: Joint Media Handling Guide, Draft 4.0.

3 Source: ethnographic fieldwork with the British military in May 2003; interview data with the British military May 2003 and October 2004.

4 Available from the MoD website: www.mod.uk/news/green_book/maintext.htm.

5 Source: interview data with the British military, November 2010.

3 The aims of Media Operations

1 The other component is categorized as 'Counter Command Activity', which seeks to attack an adversary's capabilities (JWP 3-80, 2002: 2-2)

2 Radio broadcasting, leaflets, loudspeaker messages and military-designed mini-newspapers are all categorized as Psychological Operations, which is one of the range of Influencing Activities. Commando Solo was a radio station set up by US forces in Iraq. Oksigen was a radio station set up by NATO in 1999 in post-conflict Bosnia-Herzegovina. It ceased broadcasting in 2005. Rana FM was launched by the Canadian military in 2007 in Afghanistan in support of NATO peace-building and counterinsurgency operations.

3 Source: ethnographic fieldwork with the British military, May 2003, October 2004, March 2009 and March 2010; interview data with the British military, June 2008.

4 Source: ethnographic fieldwork with the British military, March 2009 and March 2010; interview data with the British military, June 2008.
5 Source: ethnographic fieldwork with the British military, March 2009; interview data with the British military, June 2008.
6 Source: ethnographic fieldwork with the British military, March 2009, March 2010.
7 Source: ethnographic fieldwork with the British military, May 2003 and November 2001.
8 Source: ethnographic fieldwork with the British military, May 2003 and November 2001.
9 Source: interview with the British military, October 2003.
10 Similar arguments have been presented in the body of work dedicated as the CNN Effect, in which the media are believed to have a substantial, if not direct, impact on foreign policy decision-making. See, for example, Robinson (2000a, 2000b, 2001), Livingstone (1997) and Gowing (1996a, 1996b).
11 Source: ethnographic fieldwork with the British military, May 2003; interview data with the British military, May 2003 and October 2004.
12 Source: ethnographic fieldwork with the British military, May 2003; interview data with the British military, May 2003 and October 2004.

4 Media Operations: an interactionist perspective

1 Source: ethnographic fieldwork with the British military, May 2003; interview data with the British military, October 2004.

5 Audiences: imagining and influencing

1 Source: interview data with the British military, May 2003.
2 Source: ethnographic fieldwork undertaken with the British military, November 2001 and May 2003; interview data with the British military, May 2003 and October 2004.
3 Source: interview data with the British military, November 2010.
4 Source: ethnographic fieldwork undertaken with the British military, March 2010.
5 Source: ethnographic fieldwork undertaken with the British military, May 2003; interview data with the British military, October 2004.
6 Source: ethnographic fieldwork undertaken with the British military, May 2003, March 2009 and March 2010.
7 Source: ethnographic fieldwork undertaken with the British military, May 2003; interview data with the British military, October 2004.
8 Source: Interview data with the British military, October 2004, March 2009 and March 2010.
9 Source: interview data with the British military, October 2004.
10 Source: ethnographic fieldwork undertaken with the British military, March 2008 and March 2009.
11 Source: ethnographic fieldwork undertaken with the British military, May 2003.

6 Defining war: control moves

1 Source: ethnographic fieldwork undertaken with the British military, May 2003; interview data with the British military, October 2004.
2 Source: military document: Joint Media Handling Guide, Draft 4.0, obtained during ethnographic work; ethnographic fieldwork undertaken with the British military, May 2003; interview data with the British military, October 2004.
3 Source: military document: Joint Media Handling Guide, Draft 4.0, obtained during ethnographic work.
4 Source: interview data with the British military, October 2004.

5 Source: ethnographic fieldwork undertaken with the British military, May 2003.

6 Source: ethnographic fieldwork undertaken with the British military, March 2009.

7 Source: military document: Joint Media Handling Guide, Draft 4.0, obtained during ethnographic work.

8 It is noteworthy that this perceived success was in part contingent on the Iraqi regime being devoid of an air force and air power capabilities. It is also noteworthy that alternative interpretations of the same images – particularly among Arab media, especially Al Jazeera – fundamentally contradicted these intended definitions by focusing on the civilian casualties and arguing that the bombing was in fact an attack on the Iraqi people in a 'war of occupation' (Iskandar and el-Nawawy, 2004: 323). Despite this, the bombing images were still considered a success. This is perhaps indicative of how, when measuring the success of Media Operations work, the military focus on the communication, rather than interpretation, of an intended definition or image.

9 Source: ethnographic fieldwork with the British military, May 2003; interview data with the British military, May 2003 and October 2004; television data from BBC, ITV and Channel 4 News.

10 Source: ethnographic fieldwork undertaken with the British military in March 2009 and March 2010.

11 Source: interview with the British military, June 2008; MoD Communications Briefing obtained during ethnographic fieldwork with the military, November 2010.

12 Source: MoD Communications Briefing obtained during ethnographic fieldwork with the military, October 2010.

13 Source: ethnographic fieldwork with the British military, March 2009 and March 2010.

14 Source: ethnographic fieldwork with the British military, May 2003.

15 Source: quote from military member during ethnographic fieldwork with the British military, March 2009.

16 Source: ethnographic fieldwork with the British military, May 2003 and May 2004.

17 Source: Afghanistan Background Briefing, December 2009, obtained from ethnographic fieldwork work with the military, October 2010.

18 Source: ethnographic fieldwork with the British military, May 2003.

19 Source: ethnographic fieldwork with the British military, May 2003.

20 Source: interview data with the British military, November 2010.

21 More often than not it is the commander who is actively encouraged to engage with the media, not least because they embody notions of operational authority and power (JDP 3-45.1, 2007: 4-2). However, it is usually with reluctance that military officers take on a media spokesperson role, believing their operational duties to be better focused elsewhere. Once again, this is indicative of the traditional reticence that remains among military members to engage with the media. Source: ethnographic fieldwork with the British military, May 2003, May 2004 and May 2008.

22 Source: ethnographic fieldwork with the British military, May 2003 and May 2004.

23 Source: interview with the British military, May 2003; *BBC News* and *Channel 4 News*.

24 Source: interview data with the British military, May 2003.

25 Source: interview data with the British military, May, 2003.

26 Source: ethnographic fieldwork with the British military, May 2003; interview with the British military, October 2004.

27 Source: ethnographic fieldwork with the British military, May 2003.

28 Source: MoD Communications Briefing obtained during ethnographic fieldwork with the military, November 2010; interview with the British military, December 2010.

29 Source: interview with the British military, December 2010.

30 Source: interview with the British military, November 2010.

31 Source: ethnographic fieldwork with the British military, May 2003; interview with the British military, October 2004.

32 Source: ethnographic fieldwork with the British military, November 2009; interview with the British military, November 2010.

7 Defining war: strategic interaction

1 Source: ethnographic fieldwork with the British military, November 2001.
2 Source: ethnographic fieldwork with the British military, May 2003; interview data with the British military, May 2003 and October 2004.
3 Source: ethnographic fieldwork with the British military, May 2003; Interview data with the British military, May 2003 and October 2004.
4 Source: ethnographic fieldwork with the British military, May 2003; interview with the British military, October 2004.
5 Source: ethnographic fieldwork with the British military, May 2003; interview with the British military, October 2004.
6 Source: Whitehall Core Script: Afghanistan, dated November 2010, obtained during ethnographic fieldwork with the military, November 2010.
7 Source: Cross Government Background Briefing: Afghanistan, dated 2009, obtained during ethnographic fieldwork with the military, November 2010.
8 Source: ethnographic fieldwork with the British military, May 2003; interview with the British military, May 2003.
9 Source: ethnographic fieldwork with the British military, May 2003; interview with the British military, May 2003.
10 Source: ethnographic fieldwork with the British military, May 2003.
11 Source: ethnographic fieldwork with the British military, November 2001 and May 2003.
12 Source: ethnographic fieldwork with the British military, November 2001 and May 2003; interview with the British military, May 2003.
13 Source: ethnographic fieldwork undertaken with the British military, May 2003; interview data with the British military, October 2004.
14 Source: ethnographic fieldwork undertaken with the British military, May 2003; interview data with the British military, October 2004.
15 Source: ethnographic fieldwork with the British military, May 2003; interview with the British military, October 2004.
16 Source: interview with the British military, May 2003.
17 Source: ethnographic fieldwork with the British military, May 2003, March 2009 and March 2010; interview data with a British military member, October 2004.
18 Jessica Lynch became an icon of the Iraq War after the story of her capture by the Iraqis and her rescue by US Special Forces. See 'The truth about Jessica': *Guardian*, 15 May 2003.
19 Source: ethnographic fieldwork with the British military, March 2009.
20 Source: ethnographic fieldwork with the British military, March 2009.
21 Source: ethnographic fieldwork with the British military, March 2009 and March 2010.
22 Source: interview with the British military, May 2003.
23 Source: interview with the British military, May 2003.
24 It is noteworthy that these bombing definitions emanated from the wider political sphere rather than the military precisely because they were reluctant to engage with the media on such a controversial topic (see *Correspondent: War Spin*, BBC 2, 18 May 2003).

8 Performing war: bounded impression management

1 Source: ethnographic fieldwork with the British military, May 2003.
2 Source: ethnographic fieldwork with the British military, May 2003.

3 Source: ethnographic fieldwork with the British military, May 2003.
4 Source: ethnographic fieldwork with the British military, May 2003.
5 Available from MoD website: www.mod.uk/news/green_book/maintext.htm.
6 Source: ethnographic fieldwork with the British military, May 2003; interview data with the British military, October 2004.
7 Source: ethnographic fieldwork with the British military, November 2001 and May 2003.
8 Source: ethnographic fieldwork with the British military, November 2001 and May 2003.
9 Source: interview data with a British military member, May 2003.
10 Source: interview with the British military, November 2010.
11 Source: ethnographic fieldwork with the British military, November 2001 and May 2003.
12 Source: ethnographic fieldwork with the British military, November 2001 and May 2003.
13 Source: based on interviews with media personnel and a British military Media Operations staff member, May 2003.
14 Source: ethnographic fieldwork with the British military, May 2003; interview data with the British military, October 2004.

9 Performing war: distanciated impression management

1 Source: ethnographic fieldwork with the British military, May 2003; interview data with the British military, May 2003 and October 2004.
2 Source: ethnographic fieldwork with the British military, May 2003; interview data with the British military, May 2003 and October 2004.
3 Source: ethnographic fieldwork with the British military, May 2003; interview data with the British military May 2003 and October 2004; television data from *BBC News*, *ITV News* and *Channel 4 News*.
4 Source: ethnographic fieldwork with the British military, November 2001 and May 2003; interview data with the British military, May 2003.
5 Source: ethnographic fieldwork with the British military, November 2001.
6 Source: ethnographic fieldwork with the British military, November 2001 and May 2003; interview data with the British military, May 2003.
7 Source: ethnographic fieldwork with the British military, November 2001 and May 2003; interview data with the British military, May 2003.
8 Source: ethnographic fieldwork with the British military, March 2010.
9 Source: ethnographic fieldwork with the British military, March 2010.
10 Source: ethnographic fieldwork with the British military, March 2010.
11 Source: ethnographic fieldwork with the British military, March 2010.
12 Source: ethnographic fieldwork with the British military, November 2001 and May 2003.
13 Source: interview data with the British military, May 2003.
14 Source: interview data with the British military, May 2003.
15 Source: interview data with the British military, May 2003.
16 Source: ethnographic work with the British military, May 2003.

10 Impression management and mediatized war: negotiating the 'front' line

1 Tawhid Wal Jihad, under the leadership of Jordanian Abu Musab al-Zarqawi, were responsible for the beheading of Kenneth Bigley, along with Jack Hensley and Eugene Armstrong in 2004. Videos of the killings were posted on Islamist websites and on at least one US-based website specializing in violence and pornography. Prior

to the beheadings, video footage of their captivity was released and distributed through the media.

2 See, for example: 'Congo Killing Fields' (*Dispatches Documentary*, Channel 4, 19 August 2003) and 'Sri Lanka's Killing Fields' (*Dispatches Documentary*, Channel 4, 14 June 2011).

Bibliography

Adams, V. (1986) *The Media and the Falklands Campaign*. London: MacMillan.

Adler, P. and Adler, P. (1998) *Observational Techniques*. London: Sage.

Allan, S. and Zelizer, B. (eds.) (2004) *Reporting War: Journalism in Wartime*. London: Routledge.

Allen, M. and Caillouet, R. (1994) 'Legitimation endeavors: impression management strategies used by an organization in crisis'. *Communication Monographs*, 61: 44–62.

Altheide, D. (1996) *Qualitative Media Analysis*. London: Sage.

Altheide, D. and Snow, R. (1979) *Media Logic*. Beverly Hills, CA: Sage.

Andersen, R. (2006) *A Century of Media, a Century of War*. New York: Peter Lang.

Aristotle (1978) *On Politics*. London: Penguin.

Aristotle (1991) *On Rhetoric: A Theory of Civic Discourse*. Oxford: Oxford University Press.

Atkinson, P. and Coffey, A. (1997) 'Analysing documentary realities'. In D. Silverman (ed.), *Qualitative Research: Theory, Method and Practice*. London: Sage.

Badsey, S. (1994) *Modern Military Operations and the Media*. Camberley: Strategic and Combat Studies Institute.

Badsey, S. (1996) 'The influence of the media on recent British military operations'. In I. Stewart and S. Carruthers (eds.), *War, Culture and the Media: Representations of the Military in 20th Century Britain*. Wiltshire: Flick Books.

Badsey, S. (2000) 'The media, the military and public opinion'. In S. Badsey (ed.), *The Media and International Security*. London: Frank Cass Publishers.

Badsey, S. (2001) 'Guarding the media flank'. JSCSC: Advanced Command Staff Course, No 5. September 2001–July 2002.

Baudrillard, J. (1991) *La Guerre du Golfe n'a pas eu lieu*, Paris: Galilée.

Baudrillard, J. (1993a) *Symbolic Exchange and Death*. London: Sage.

Baudrillard, J. (1993b) *The Transparency of Evil: Essays on Extreme Phenomena*. London: Verso.

Baudrillard, J. (1995) *The Gulf War Did Not Take Place*. Bloomington, IN: Indiana University Press.

Bauman, Z. (1997) *Postmodernity and its Discontents*. New York: New York University Press.

Berelson, B., Lazarsfeld, P. and McPhee, W. (1954) *Voting: A Study of Opinion Formation in a Presidential Campaign*. Chicago, IL: University of Chicago Press.

Blumer, H. (1962) 'Society as symbolic interaction'. In A. Rose (ed.), *Human Behaviour and Social Processes*. London: Routledge.

Blumer, H. (1969) *Symbolic Interactionism: Perspective and Method*. Englewood Cliffs, NJ: Prentice-Hall.

Blumer, J. (1990) 'Elections, the media and the modern publicity process'. In M. Ferguson (ed.), *Public Communication: The New Imperatives*. London: Sage.

Blumler, J. and Kavanagh, D. (1999) 'The third age of political communication: influences and features'. *Political Communication*, 16: 209–230.

Bracken, M. (2009) *Military Media Interaction*. Unpublished Masters Dissertation submitted to City University, Summer 2009.

Braestrup, P. (1983) *Big Story: How the American Press and Television Reported and Interpreted the Crisis of Tet, 1968, in Vietnam and Washington*. London: Yale University Press.

Brauman, R. (1993) 'When suffering makes a good story'. In M.S. Frontières (ed.), *Life, Death and Aid*. London: Routledge and Hachette.

Brown, P. and Levison, S. (1987) *Studies in Interactional Sociolinguistics: Vol. 4. Politeness: Some Universals in Language Use*. Cambridge: Cambridge University Press.

Brown, S. (1993) *Crime and Law in Media Culture*. Buckingham: Open University Press.

Burns, J. (1996) 'Media as impartial observers or protagonists'. In J. Gow, R. Paterson and A. Preston (eds.), *Bosnia by Television*. London: BFI.

Burrell, G. and Morgan, G. (1979) *Sociological Paradigms and Organisational Analysis*. London: Heinemann.

Carruthers, S. (2000) *The Media at War: Communications and Conflict in the 20th Century*. London: Macmillan.

Castells, M. (2000) 'Materials for an explanatory theory of the network society'. *British Journal of Sociology*, 51 (1): 5–24.

Castells, M. (2009) *Communication Power*. Oxford: Oxford University Press.

Chibnall, S. (1977) *Law and Order News*. London: Tavistock.

Clausewitz, C. (1997 [1832]) *On War*. Hertfordshire: Wordsworth Editions Ltd.

Cottle, S. (2006) *Mediatized Conflict*. Berkshire: Open University Press.

Cottle, S. (2008) *Global Crisis Reporting*. Berkshire: Open University Press.

Couldry, N. and Downing, J. (2004) 'War or peace? Legitimation, dissent, and rhetorical closure in press coverage of the Iraq war build-up'. In S. Allan and B. Zelizer (eds.), *Reporting War: Journalism in Wartime*. London: Routledge.

Cummings, B. (1992) *War and Television*. London: Verso.

Dandeker, C. (2000) 'The United Kingdom: the overstretched military'. In C. Moskos, J. Williams and R. Segal (eds.), *The Postmodern Military: Armed Forces After the Cold War*. Oxford: Oxford University Press.

Davies, C. (1999) *Reflexive Ethnography*. London: Routledge.

Deutscher, I. (1973) *What We Say/What We Do: Sentiments and Acts*. Glenview, IL: Scott, Foresman.

Diamond, E. and Bates, S. (1984) *The Spot: The Use of Political Advertising on Television*. Cambridge, MA: MIT Press.

Downey, J. and Murdock, G. (2003) 'The counter revolution in military affairs: the globalization of guerrilla warfare'. In D. Kishan Thussu and D. Freedman (eds.), *War and the Media*. London: Sage.

Doyle, A. (2003) *Arresting Images: Crime and Policing in Front of the Television Camera*. Toronto: University of Toronto Press.

Edelmen, M. (1964) *The Symbolic Uses of Politics*. Urbana, IL: University of Illinois Press.

Ericson, R., Baranek, P. and Chan, J. (1989) *Negotiating Control: A Study of News Sources*. Milton Keynes: Open University Press.

Ericson, R., Baranek, P. and Chan, J. (1991) *Representing Order*. Toronto: Open University Press.

Espinosa, P. (1982) 'The audience in text: ethnographic observations of a Hollywood conference'. *Media Culture and Society*, 4: 77–86.

Fielding, N. (1993) 'Ethnography'. In N. Gilbert (ed.), *Researching Social Life*. London: Sage.

Fishman, M. (1980) *Manufacturing the News*. London: University of Texas Press.

Fiske, J. (1987) *Television Culture*. London: Routledge.

Foster, K. (1992) 'The Falklands War: a critical view of information policy'. In P. Young (ed.) *Defence and the Media in Time of Limited War*. London: Cassell.

Garfinkel, A. (1967) *Studies in Ethnomethodology*. Englewood Cliffs, NJ: Prentice-Hall.

Giddens, A. (1988a) 'Goffman as a systematic social theorist'. In P. Drew and A. Wooton (eds.), *Erving Goffman: Exploring the Interaction Order*. Cambridge: Polity.

Giddens, A. (1998b) *The Third Way: The Renewal of Social Democracy*. Cambridge: Polity.

Gill, R. (1993) 'Ideology, gender and popular radio: a discourse analytic approach'. *Innovation*, 6: 323–339.

Gillespie, M. (2006) 'Security, media, legitimacy: multi-ethnic media publics and the Iraq War 2003', *International Relations*, 20 (4): 467–486.

Gitlin, T. (1980) *The Whole World is Watching*. Berkeley, CA: University of California Press.

Glasgow University Media Group (1985) *War and Peace News*. Milton Keynes: Open University Press.

Goffman, E. (1959) *The Presentation of Self in Everyday Life*. New York: Doubleday.

Goffman, E. (1963) *Stigma: Notes on the Management of a Spoiled Identity*. London: Penguin.

Goffman, E. (1967) *Interaction Ritual*. New York: Pantheon Books.

Goffman, E. (1969) *Strategic Interaction*. Oxford: Basil Blackwell.

Gold, R. L. (1958) 'Roles in sociological field observation'. *Social Forces*, 36: 217–223.

Gouldner, A. (1970) *The Coming Crisis of Western Sociology*. New York: Basic Books.

Gowing, N. (1996a) 'The tyranny of real time'. *Journal of the Territorial Army Pool of Public Information Officers*, 6: 61–64.

Gowing, N. (1996b) 'Real-time TV coverage from war: does it make or break government policy?'. In J. Gow, R. Paterson and A. Preston (eds.), *Bosnia by Television*. London: BFI Publishing.

Green Book, The (2003) *British Military Guidelines for Working with Media Organisations During Operations*. www.mod.uk/news/green_book/maintext.htm (downloaded May 2003).

Green Book, The (2006) *British Military Guidelines for Working with Media Organisations During Operations*. www.mod.uk/NR/rdonlyres/36DBFDCE-6739-4DB3-B589-7162FCA85B25/0/mod_green_book_20051130.pdf (downloaded March 2006).

Green Book, The (2010) *British Military Guidelines for Working with Media Organisations During Operations*. Version 7. Sourced from the British Military.

Hall, R. (1972) *Organisations: Structures, Processes and Outcomes* (6th edn.). New Jersey: Prentice-Hall.

Hall, S., Critcher, C., Jefferson, T., Clarke, J. and Roberts, B. (1978) *Policing the Crisis: Mugging the State and Law and Order*. London: Macmillan Press.

Hallin, D. (1989) *The 'Uncensored War': The Media and Vietnam*. London: University of California Press.

Hammersley, M. and Atkinson, P. (1995) *Ethnography: Principles in Practice*. London: Routledge.

Hanson, N. (1958) *Patterns of Discovery*. London: Cambridge University Press.

Hirst, P. (2001) *War and Power in the 21st Century*. Cambridge: Polity.

Hjarvard, S. (2004) 'From bricks to bytes: the mediatization of a global toy industry'. In I. Bondebjerg and P. Golding (eds.), *European Culture and the Media*. Bristol: Intellect Press.

Hjarvard, S. (2007) 'Sprogets medialisering' [The mediatization of language]. In *Språk i Norden 2007*. Oslo: Nettverket for språknemndene i Norden.

Hjarvard, S. (2008a) 'The mediatization of society: a theory of media as agents of social and cultural change'. *Nordicom Review*, 29 (2): 105–134.

Hjarvard, S. (2008b) 'The mediatization of religion'. In *Northern Lights 2008*. Bristol: Intellect Press.

Hoskins, A. (2004) *Televising War: From Vietnam to Iraq*. London: Continuum.

Hoskins, A. and O'Loughlin, B. (2007) *Television and Terror: Conflicting Times and the Crisis of News Discourse. New Security Challenges*. Basingstoke: Palgrave Macmillan.

Hoskins, A. and O'Loughlin, B. (2010) *War and Media: The Emergence of Diffused War*. Cambridge: Polity.

Iskandar, A. and El-Nawawy, N. (2004) 'Al-Jazeera and war coverage in Iraq: the media's quest for contextual objectivity'. In S. Allan and B. Zelizer (eds.), *Reporting War: Journalism in Wartime*. London: Routledge.

Jackson, M. (2007) *Solider: An Autobiography*. London: Bantam Press.

Janowitz, M. (1971) *The Professional Soldier: A Social and Political Portrait*. New York: Free Press.

JDP (Joint Doctrine Publication) (2007) *3-45.1: Media Operations*. Joint Doctrine and Concepts Centre (JDCC). www.mod.uk/DefenceInternet/AboutDefence/CorporatePublications/DoctrineOperationsandDiplomacyPublications/JWP/Jwp345MediaOperations.htm (accessed August 2007).

JDP (2008) *0-01: British Defence Doctrine* (3rd edn.). Joint Doctrine and Concepts Centre (JDCC). www.mod.uk/DefenceInternet/MicroSite/DCDC/OurPublications/JDWP/JointDoctrinePublicationjdp001BritishDefenceDoctrine.htm (accessed May 2008).

JDP (2009) *3-40: Security and Stabilisation: The Military Contribution*. Joint Doctrine and Concepts Centre (JDCC). www.mod.uk/DefenceInternet/MicroSite/DCDC/OurPublications/JDWP/Jdp340SecurityAndStabilisationTheMilitaryContribution.htm (accessed August 2009).

Johansson, C. (2009) 'On Goffman: researching relations with Erving Goffman as pathfinder'. In O. Ihlen, B. van Ruler and M. Fredrickson (eds.), *Public Relations and Social Theory: Key Figures and Concepts*. London: Routledge.

Juergensmeyer, M. (2000) *Terror in the Mind of God: The Global Rise of Religious Violence*. Berkeley, CA: University of California Press.

JWP (Joint Warfare Publication) (2001) *3-45: Media Operations*. Joint Doctrine and Concepts Centre (JDCC). www.mod.uk/DefenceInternet/AboutDefence/CorporatePublications/DoctrineOperationsandDiplomacyPublications/JWP/Jwp345MediaOperations.htm (accessed August 2003).

JWP (2002) *3-80: Information Operations*. Joint Doctrine and Concepts Centre (JDCC). www.mod.uk/linked_files/jdcc/publications/jwp3_80.pdf (accessed August 2003).

Keeble, R. (2004) 'Information warfare in an age of hyper-militarism'. In S. Allan and B. Zelizer (eds.), *Reporting War: Journalism in Wartime*. London: Routledge.

Keeble, R. and Mair, J. (2010) *Afghanistan, War and Media: Deadlines and Frontlines*. Bury St Edmunds: Arima Publishing.

Kellner, D. (1992) *The Persian Gulf TV War*. Boulder, CO: Westview Press.

Kraus, S. and Davis, D. (1976) *The Effects of Mass Communication on Political Behaviour*. University Park: Pennsylvania State University Press.

Krotz, F. (2007) *Mediatisierung: Fallstudien zum Wandel von Kommunikation*. Wiesbaden: VS Verlag für Socialwissenschaften.

Laqueur, W. (1977) *Guerrilla: A Historical and Critical Study*. London: Weidenfeld and Nicolson.

Lawrence, P. and Lorsch, J. (1967) *Organisation and Environment*. Cambridge, MA: Harvard University Press.

Levi Strauss, C. (1978) *Myth and Meaning*. London: Routledge and Kegan Paul.

Lewis, J. and Brookes, R. (2004) 'How British television news represented the case for the Iraq war'. In S. Allan and B. Zelizer (eds.), *Reporting War: Journalism in Wartime*. London: Routledge.

Libicki, M. (1995) *What is Information Warfare?* Washington, DC: National Defense University Press.

Livingston, S. (1997) *Clarifying the CNN Effect: An Examination of Media Effects According to Type of Military Intervention*. Cambridge, MA: The Joan Shorenstein Center, Harvard University.

Livingstone, S. (2009a) 'On the mediation of everything: ICA presidential address 2008'. *Journal of Communication*, 59: 1–18.

Livingstone, S. (2009b) 'Coming to terms with mediatization'. In K. Lundby (ed.), *Mediatization: Concepts, Changes, Consequences*. New York: Peter Lang.

Lofland, J. and Lofland, L. (1995) *Analysing Social Settings: A Guide to Qualitative Observation and Analysis*. Belmont: Wadsworth Publishing Company.

Lundby, K. (2009) 'Mediatization as key'. In K. Lundby (ed.), *Mediatization: Concepts, Changes, Consequences*. New York: Peter Lang.

McLaughlin, G. (2002) *The War Correspondent*. London: Pluto Press.

McQuail, D. (2006) 'On the mediatization of war: a review article'. *The International Communication Gazette*, 68 (2): 107–118.

Maltby, S. (2007) 'Communicating war: strategies and implications'. In S. Maltby and R. Keeble (eds.), *Communicating War: Memory, Media and Military*. Bury St Edmunds: Arima Publishing.

Maltby, S. (2010) 'Mediating peace? Military influencing activities in the Balkans and Afghanistan'. In R. Keeble, J. Tulloch and F. Zollman (eds.), *Journalism, War and Conflict Resolution*. New York: Peter Lang.

Manning, P. (2003) *Policing Contingencies*. London: University of Chicago Press.

May, T. (2001) *Social Research: Issues, Methods and Process*. Buckingham: Open University Press.

Mazzoleni, G. (2008a) 'Media logic'. In W. Donsbach (ed.), *The International Encyclopedia of Communication*, vol. VII. Malden: Blackwell.

Mazzoleni, G. (2008b) 'Mediatization of politics'. In W. Donsbach (ed.), *The International Encyclopedia of Communication*, vol. VII. Malden: Blackwell.

Mazzoleni, G. and Schulz, W. (1999) 'Mediatization of politics: a challenge for democracy'. *Political Communication*, 16: 247–261.

Mead, G. (1967) *Mind, Self and Society*. Chicago, IL: University of Chicago Press.

Metzler, M. (2001) 'The centrality of organizational legitimacy to public relations practice'. In R. Heath and G. Vasquez (eds.), *Handbook of Public Relations*. Thousand Oaks, CA: Sage.

Meyrowitz, J. (1985) *No Sense of Place: The Impact of Electronic Media on Behaviour*. Oxford: Oxford University Press.

Miller, D. (2004) *Tell Me Lies: Propaganda and Media Distortion in the Attack on Iraq*. London: Pluto.

Moeller, S. (1999) *Compassion Fatigue: How the Media Sell Disease, Famine, War and Death*. New York: Routledge.

Molander, R., Riddile, A. and Wilson, P. (1996) *Strategic Information Management: A New Face of War*. Santa Monica, CA: RAND.

Molotch, H. and Lester, M. (1974) 'News as purposive behaviour'. *American Sociological Review*, 39: 101–112.

Moorcroft, P. and Taylor, P. (2008) *Shooting the Messenger: The Political Impact of War Reporting*. Washington, DC: Potomac.

Morrison, D. (1994) 'Journalists and the social construction of war'. *Contemporary Record*, 8 (2): 305–320.

Morrison, D. and Tumber, H. (1988) *Journalists at War: The Dynamics of News Reporting During the Falklands Conflict*. London: Sage.

Moskos, C. (1992) 'Armed forces in a warless society'. *Forum International*, 13: 3–10.

Negrine, R. and Stanyer, J. (2007) 'Introduction'. In R. Negrine and J. Stanyer (eds.), *The Political Communication Reader*. Oxford: Oxford University Press.

Paletz, D. and Schmid, A. (eds.) (1992) *Terrorism and the Media*. London: Sage.

Parsons, T. (1959) *Economy and Society*. London: Routledge and Kegan Paul.

Patton, M. (1990) *Qualitative Evaluation and Research Methods*. Newbury Park: Sage.

Pekurny, R. (1982) 'Coping with television production'. In J. Ettema and S. Whitney (eds.), *Individuals in Mass Media Organisations: Creativity and Constraint*. Beverley Hills, CA: Sage.

Peri, Y. (2006) *Generals in the Cabinet Room: How the Military Shapes Israeli Policy*. Washington, DC: United States Institute of Peace.

Perrow, C. (1961) 'The Analysis of Goals in Complex Organizations'. *American Sociological Review*, 26: 688–699.

Propp, V. (1968) *Morphology of the Folktale* (2nd edn.). Austin, TX: University of Texas Press.

Rid, T. (2007) *War and Media Operations: The U.S. Military and the Press from Vietnam to Iraq*. London: Routledge.

Robinson, P. (2000a) 'The news media and intervention: triggering the use of air power during humanitarian crisis'. *European Journal of Communication*, 15 (3): 405–414.

Robinson, P. (2000b) 'The policy–media interaction model: measuring media power during humanitarian crisis'. *Peace Research*, 37(5): 613–633.

Robinson, P. (2001) 'Operation Restore Hope and the illusion of a news media driven intervention'. *Political Studies*, 49: 941–956.

Robinson, P., Goddard, P., Parry, P., Murray, C. and Taylor, P. (2010) *Pockets of Resistance: British News Media, War and Theory in the 2003 Invasion of Iraq*. Manchester: Manchester University Press.

Rogers, Mary F. (1980) 'Goffman on power, hierarchy, and status'. In J. Ditton (ed.), *The View from Goffman*. London: Sage.

Sanders, K. (2009) *Communicating Politics in the Twenty-first Century*. Basingstoke: Palgrave Macmillan.

Schechter, D. (2003) *Embedded: Weapons of Mass Deception. How the Media Failed to Cover the War in Iraq*. New York: News Dissector/Mediachannel.org.

Scheff, T. (2005) 'Looking-glass self: Goffman as symbolic interactionist'. *Symbolic Interaction*, 28 (2): 147–166.

Schlesinger, P. and Tumber, H. (1994) *Reporting Crime: The Media of Politics and Criminal Justice*. Oxford: Oxford University Press.

Schmid, A. and De Graaf, J. (1982) *Violence as Communication*. London: Sage.

Schrott, Andrea (2009) 'Dimensions: catch-all label or technical term'. In K. Lundby (ed.), *Mediatization: Concepts, Changes, Consequences*. New York: Peter Lang.

Schulz, W. (2004) 'Reconstructing mediatization as an analytical concept', *European Journal of Communication*, 19 (1): 87–101.

Schwartau, W. (1994) *Information Warfare: Chaos on the Electronic Superhighway*. New York: Thunder's Mouth Press.

Shaw, M. (1996) *Civil Society and Media in a Global Crisis: Representing Distant Violence*. London: Pinter.

Shibutani, T. (1966) *Improvised News: A Sociological Study of Rumour*. New York: Bobbs-Merrill.

Silverstone, R. (2005) 'The sociology of mediation and communication'. In C. Calhoun, B. Rojek and B. Turner (eds.), *The Sage Handbook of Sociology*. London: Sage.

Smith, G. (1999) 'Interpreting Goffman's sociological legacy'. In G. Smith (eds.), *Goffman and Social Organisation: Studies in a Sociological Legacy.* London: Routledge.

Smith, G. (2006) *Erving Goffman*. London: Routledge.

Strategic Defence Review (1998) HM government.

Swanson, D. (1997) 'The political–media complex at 50: putting the 1996 presidential campaign in context'. *American Behavioral Scientist*, 40 (8): 1264–1282.

Swanson, D. and Mancini, P. (1996) 'Patterns of modern electoral campaigning and their consequences'. In D. Swanson and P. Mancini (eds.), *Politics, Media and Modern Democracy.* Westport, CT: Praeger.

Tatham, S. (2006) *Losing Arab Hearts and Minds: The Coalition, Al Jazeera and Muslim Public Opinion*. London: Hurst and Company.

Taverner, A. (2007) 'Dimensions of perception: shaping the British approach to information strategy during military operations'. In S. Maltby and R. Keeble (eds.), *Communicating War: Memory, Media and Military*. Bury St Edmunds: Arima Publishing.

Taylor, P. (1992) *War and the Media*. Manchester: Manchester University Press.

Taylor, P. (1996) 'War and the media'. *Dispatches: The Journal for the Territorial Army Pool of Public Information Officers*, 6: 105–119.

Taylor, P. (2000) 'The military and the media: past, present and future'. In S. Badsey (ed.), *The Media and International Security*. London: Frank Cass Publishers.

Taylor, P. (2003) *Conflict and Conflicting Cultures: The Military and the Media*. Paper presented at The Role of the Media in Public Scrutiny and the Democratic Oversight of the Security Sector, Budapest, 6–9 February.

Thomson, J. (1995) *The Media and Modernity*. Cambridge: Polity.

Thrall, T. (2000) *War in the Media Age*. Cresskill, NJ: Hampton Press.

Thussu, D. and Freedman, D. (eds.) (2003) *War and the Media*. London: Sage.

Tiger Aspect Productions (2007) *Ross Kemp in Afghanistan*. Broadcast on Sky One January 2008.

Tiger Aspect Productions (2008) *Ross Kemp Return to Afghanistan*. Broadcast on Sky One, February 2009.

Todorov, T. (1988) *Literature and Its Theorists*. London: Routledge.

Toffler, A. (1991) *Powershift: Knowledge, Wealth and Violence at the Edge of the 21st Century*. New York. Bantam Books.

Toffler, A. and Toffler, H. (1980) *The Third Wave*. New York. Bantam Books.

Tuman, J. (2003) *Communicating Terror: The Rhetorical Dimensions of Terrorism*. London: Sage.

Tumber, H. (2003) 'Reporting under fire'. In B. Zelizer and S. Allan (eds.), *Journalism after September 11th*. London: Routledge.

Tumber, H. and Palmer, J. (2004) *Media at War: The Iraq Crisis*. London: Sage.

Tumber, H. and Webster, F. (2006) *Journalists Under Fire: Information War and Journalistic Practice*. London: Sage.

Väliverronen, E. (2001) 'From mediation to mediatization: the new politics of communicating science and biotechnology'. In U. Kivikuru and T. Savolainen (eds.), *The Politics of Public Issues*. Helsinki: Department of Communication, University of Helsinki.

Vasquez, G. and Taylor, M. (2000) 'Public relations: an emerging social science enters the new millennium'. In W. Gudykunst (ed.), *Communication Yearbook*, vol. 24. Thousand Oaks, CA: Sage.

Ventre, D. (2009) *Information Warfare*. London: Wiley and Sons.

Verhoeven, J. (1993) 'An interview with Erving Goffman, 1980'. *Research on Language and Social Interaction*, 26: 317–348.

Virillio, P. (1994) *The Vision Machine*. London: BFI.

Waeraas, A. (2007) 'The re-enchantment of social institutions: Max Weber and public relations'. *Public Relations Review*, 33 (3): 281–286.

Waeraas, A. (2009) 'On Weber: legitimacy and legitimation in public relations'. In O. Ihlen, B. van Ruler and M. Fredrickson (eds.), *Public Relations and Social Theory: Key Figures and Concepts*. London: Routledge.

Wight, M. (1979) 'Power politics'. In H. Bull and C. Holbraad (eds.), *Power Politics*. Harmondsworth: Penguin.

Wilcox, D. (2005) *Propaganda, the Press and Conflict: The Gulf War and Kosovo*. London: Routledge.

Index

Page numbers in *italics* denote tables, those in **bold** denote figures.